Scholarly Publishing in an Electronic Era

Scholarly Publishing in an Electronic Era

Edited by

G. E. Gorman
School of Information Management,
Victoria University of Wellington

Associate Editor
Fytton Rowland
Department of Information Science,
Loughborough University

facet publishing

© This compilation: G. E. Gorman 2005
The articles: The contributors 2005

Published by
Facet Publishing
7 Ridgmount Street
London WC1E 7AE

Facet Publishing is wholly owned by CILIP: the Chartered Institute of Library and Information Professionals.

The editor and authors of the individual chapters assert their moral right to be identified as such in accordance with the terms of the Copyright, Designs and Patents Act, 1988.

Except as otherwise permitted under the Copyright Designs and Patents Act 1988 this publication may only be reproduced, stored or transmitted in any form or by any means, with the prior permission of the publisher, or, in the case of reprographic reproduction, in accordance with the terms of a licence issued by The Copyright Licensing Agency. Enquiries concerning reproduction outside those terms should be sent to Facet Publishing, 7 Ridgmount Street, London WC1E 7AE.

First published 2005

British Library Cataloguing in Publication Data

A catalogue record for this book is available from the British Library.

ISBN 1-85604-536-6

Typeset from editor's disks by Facet Publishing in 10.5/14.5pt New Baskerville and Franklin Gothic Condensed.
Printed and made in Great Britain by MPG Books Ltd, Bodmin, Cornwall.

Contents

Editorial Advisory Board 2004/2005

Australasia

- **Dr Peter Clayton**, School of Information Management and Tourism, University of Canberra, Canberra 2601, Australia.
  E-mail: peter.clayton@canberra.edu.au

East Asia

- **Professor Schubert Foo**, Division of Information Studies, School of Communication and Information, Nanyang Technological University, Nanyang Link, Singapore.
  E-mail: assfoo@ntu.edu.sg
- **Dr Jianzhong Wu**, The Shanghai Library, 1555 Huai Hai Zhong Lu, Shanghai 200031, China.
  E-mail: jzwu@libnet.sh.cn

South Asia

- **Dr M. P. Satija**, Department of Library and Information Science, Guru Nanak Dev University, Amritsar 143005, India.
  E-mail: satija_mp@yahoo.com

About the contributors

Dr Gobinda G. Chowdhury is a senior lecturer and Director of the MSc Information Management Course in the Department of Computer and Information Sciences at the University of Strathclyde in Scotland. He has been engaged in teaching and research in different areas of information science for two decades and has worked in different parts of the world including Asia, Africa and Europe. His current research interests include information organization and access in digital libraries. He has an extensive list of publications that include eight books and over 80 papers in refereed journals and international conferences.

John Cox qualified as a barrister but has spent over 35 years in publishing, with The Open University, Butterworths and Scholastic. He joined Blackwell in 1990 as head of the subscription agency and then as Managing Director. He was Managing Director of Carfax, a UK journal publisher, from 1994. He left Carfax when it became part of Taylor & Francis in November 1998 to set up his own consultancy, John Cox Associates Ltd, which specializes in scholarly and research publishing.

Louise Edwards is a senior manager of Cranfield Information and Library Services and responsible for information services in the Cranfield School of Management, one of Europe's leading university management schools. Seconded to the Joint Information Systems Committee (JISC) from 2001 to 2003, Louise focused on the strategic development of e-books as a national resource for UK higher and further education. She has published a number of articles and presented at international conferences on the subject of e-books. At Cranfield, she has been involved in research and consultancy projects, including a nationally funded study of the economics of scholarly journals (with Dr Frank Fishwick) and an in-depth analysis of the information behaviour of management researchers in their use of journals, published as the MANDOC study.

Dr G. E. Gorman is Professor of Library and Information Management in the School of Information Management at Victoria University of Wellington. He is the founding general editor of the *International Yearbook of Library and Information Management* and the author or co-author of more than a dozen books and more than 100 refereed journal articles. He is also editor of *Online Information Review* (Emerald), Associate Editor of *Library Collections, Acquisitions and Technical Services* (Elsevier), a member of the editorial boards of several other journals, and currently Chair of IFLA's Regional Standing Committee for Asia and Oceania.

Dr John Houghton is currently Professorial Fellow at the Victoria University (Melbourne) Centre for Strategic Economic Studies and Director of the Centre's Information Technologies and the Information Economy Program. He has a number of years' experience in information and communication technology policy, science and technology policy and more general industry policy-related economic research. Prior to joining Victoria University John held the positions of: Senior Research Fellow at the Centre for International Research on Communication and Information Technologies; Principal Economist at the Bureau of Industry Economics; Adviser, Information Industries Policy at the Australian Commonwealth Department of Industry, Science and Tourism; and Principal Adviser, State Development Policy at the Victorian Department of State Development. In 1998 he was awarded an Australia Day Medal for his contribution to IT industry policy development. Dr Houghton has been actively involved in a number of professional and industry bodies, has published and spoken widely and is a regular consultant to the OECD.

Stephen Pinfield is Assistant Director of Information Services at the University of Nottingham. He is Director of the SHERPA institutional repository project and a member of the Consortium of University Research Libraries (CURL) and Society for College, National and University Libraries (SCONUL) groups on scholarly communication. He wishes to acknowledge the useful comments of Bill Hubbard on drafts of his chapter.

Dr David C. Prosser was appointed the first director of SPARC Europe in October 2002. Previously, he spent ten years in science, technical and medical journal publishing for both Oxford University Press and Elsevier Science. During this time he was involved in all aspects of publishing, from production through to editorial and financial management of journals. Before becoming a publisher he received a PhD and BSc in physics from Leeds University.

Dr Fytton Rowland originally trained as a biochemist, and then worked for many years in scientific publishing and information retrieval services work for learned societies. As Publications Production Manager at the Royal Society of Chemistry (RSC) in the mid-1980s, he took responsibility for providing the RSC's journals in electronic form to the Chemical Journals Online service run by the American Chemical Society. He has been a member of the Department of Information Science at Loughborough University since 1989 and is now a senior lecturer there. His research interests are in human and economic issues concerned with electronic scholarly publishing. His research has been funded by the British Library Research and Innovation Centre, Ingenta, the Association of Subscription Agencies and Intermediaries, and the Joint Information Systems Committee.

Dr Peter T. Shepherd has gained experience, over a 20-year career with Wiley, Pergamon, Elsevier and Harcourt, in all aspects of STM journal, book and database publishing. Dr Shepherd is now an independent publishing consultant. Since 2002 he has been Project Director of COUNTER, an international initiative to improve the reliability of online usage statistics. Release 1 of the COUNTER Code of Practice was published in January 2003 and a draft of Release 2 was published for comment in April 2004.

Colin Steele is Emeritus Fellow of the Australian National University. He was University Librarian from 1980 to 2002 and Director Scholarly Information Strategies in 2002–3. He is the author or editor of seven books and over 300 articles and reviews, including *Major Libraries of the World* (1976). He has been a keynote speaker at conferences in a number of countries including the USA, UK, China and South Africa.

Dr Alicia Wise is Chief Executive of the Publishers Licensing Society (UK). Prior to taking up this appointment, she was Collections Manager for the Joint Information Systems Committee of the UK (JISC) Further and Higher Education Funding Councils. Her background is in computer applications in the humanities, digital preservation and electronic collection development and management.

Introduction

Each year the *International Yearbook of Library and Information Management* focuses on a theme, which its expert authors address from a variety of perspectives. Past volumes have dealt with collection management, information services in an electronic environment, digitization, and metadata. Underpinning all of these earlier themes is the publishing industry, and in particular scholarly publishing. Without published products (however defined) we would have nothing to manage, process or service. We tend to think of publishing as a relatively staid, conservative enterprise, but delving beneath this superficial assessment shows that it has become extremely dynamic and surprisingly evolutionary – rather like riding a roller coaster according to some, or perhaps like visiting a chamber of horrors to others.

This new-found dynamism is in part a reaction to change in other sectors, especially technology, and to the growing global competitiveness of major publishing groups based in Britain, Germany and the USA. Interestingly, this very dynamism has caused several potential authors to shy away from committing their views to paper. As one noted authority said, 'Whatever I say today about scholarly publishing will be proved wrong tomorrow.' And that is precisely why this volume is needed: to show us where we are at the moment, to bring together the views of key experts so that we can more readily track the inevitable changes, and perhaps to engage in more meaningful dialogue along the way.

Part 1
Overview of scholarly publishing in the 21st century

This year coverage of the topic is arranged in four parts. The first of these, an overview section setting out the principal issues and indicating their significance, contains chapters by two well-known specialists, Dr Fytton Rowland (Associate Editor for the volume) of Loughborough University and Dr Alicia Wise, who has recently joined the Publishers Licensing Agency (UK). In 'Where is scholarly publishing going?' Dr Rowland characterizes traditional scholarly publishing as change resistant, but nevertheless in recent years affected by some powerful change agents, including technological and commercial factors. Once we passed through the 1990s and the continuing resistance to effective change, a number of initiatives began to evolve, and Rowland characterizes these as library consortia with the ability to stand up to publishers, new pricing structures initiated by the publishers, usage-based subscriptions and open access (this last approach may said to be a sub-theme of the volume, as it is discussed in several of the chapters). He concludes with a series of 'radical alternatives' that bear close scrutiny, for they seem less radical and more plausible with each passing day.

Complementing Chapter 1 is Dr Wise's 'Collaborative transformations in scholarly publishing', which takes a somewhat more iconoclastic view of the situation, or perhaps it is 'the view from the dark side' (her phrase, not mine). In her opinion the current debate about scholarly publishing and access to scholarly literature has enhanced the profile of publishers and information professionals with key stakeholders in academia, government and funding agencies. Although this higher profile is beneficial, the downside is that the information professions are 'at considerable risk of being written off as finger-pointing whiners who can not organise ourselves out of a tricky position'. In fact, she says, as the information chain evolves into a new model, we are finding that librarians and publishers have a great deal in common, and many benefits to derive from collaboration in meeting the challenges of scholarly publishing. Chapter 2, then, focuses on what Dr Wise sees as a shared challenge in terms of such issues as copyright, collaboration in 'e-everything', preservation, and so on. By working together, according to Wise, the entire information industry can create a more effective and positive relationship that benefits everyone.

Part 2
Institutional perspectives on scholarly publishing

This leads us neatly to Part 2, which offers an alternative to Dr Wise's picture of an industry learning to move forward as a single, collaborative unit. Indeed, the two perspectives represented here – the librarian's and the publisher's – suggest that the traditional differences may remain, and that genuine, trusting collaboration is some way off. Writing for the library community, an early apostle of the virtual library, Colin Steele (former University Librarian at the Australian National University) offers us 'The library's perspective on scholarly publishing in the 21st century' (Chapter 3). He maintains that the traditional role of libraries as collectors and storers of scholarly information is changing as knowledge production is transformed by digital technology. Within universities in particular there are emerging new models of collaboration for accessing and storing scholarly information. At the same time, the libraries themselves are becoming involved in the production and distribution of scholarly information, using institutional repository schemes and open access initiatives. All of this is seen as an alternative, or an addition, to the role and place of external scholarly publishers, and something that many publishers view with some suspicion, or at least a degree of anxiety.

John Cox, with his long experience in the publishing industry, looks at issues somewhat differently in Chapter 4, 'Evolution or revolution in scholarly publishing: challenges to the publisher'. As he sees it, the gap between the ever-growing volume of scholarly literature and available library budgets continues to widen. The 'Big Deal', an early attempt to close that gap by offering much more content for a small cost increase, has come in for much criticism – clear evidence that the market for scholarly information online is still evolving. Beyond these general trends, Cox concentrates on two developments as exemplars of the current unrest in the scholarly publishing community: the collapse of RoweCom and the challenge presented by open access to conventional STM publishing. Based on these examples, Cox sets out some important lessons to be learned, and raises a number of unsettling questions that await answers as the scene continues to unfold.

Part 3
Access and preservation initiatives in scholarly publishing

In Chapter 5 ('Access and usability issues of scholarly electronic publications'), Dr Gobinda Chowdhury of Strathclyde University discusses access and usability issues related to scholarly information resources. He is especially concerned with issues and studies surrounding usability and user friendliness, and identifies some important parameters for measuring the usability of information access systems. Finally, he outlines major problems that hybrid library users face in gaining access to scholarly information, and mentions some possible measures to resolve these problems, one of which may well be open access.

Enter Dr David Prosser (SPARC Europe), who in Chapter 6 writes on 'The next information revolution: how open access will transform scholarly communications'. Prosser begins with a summary of the all-too-common complaints lodged by librarians and researchers, and moves on to discuss new models under development that better serve the information needs of academics as both authors and readers. This includes the ability of authors to 'self-archive' their work, making it available to anyone who cares to read it, and new open access journals extend this by providing a peer-review service to ensure quality control. This is what he sees as the emerging scholarly communication landscape, mediated by open access. In Prosser's words,

> SPARC and SPARC Europe play a prominent role in the new scholarly communication landscape as they encourage the progress of open access while working closely with scholars and scientists, who must recognize the benefits of change within academe in order for such progress to occur.

Stephen Pinfield's 'Self-archiving publications' (Chapter 7) picks up the idea of self-archiving publications and makes this the theme of his entire chapter. He discusses the historical development, current practice and future prospects of the self-archiving of research papers in open access repositories or 'e-print archives'. Experience has shown that self-archiving can benefit academic researchers (and potentially others) by enabling quick and easy access to the research literature, thereby maximizing the potential impact of papers. Realizing that the possible benefits are high and the technical entry barriers low, many organizations such as universities have recently tried to encourage widespread self-archiving by setting up institutional repositories. However, major barriers to self-archiving remain – most of them cultural and managerial. There are concerns about quality control, intellectual property rights, disturbing the publishing status quo, and workload. Ways in which these issues are currently being addressed are discussed in Pinfield's chapter. However, many unresolved issues remain, and of these Pinfield discusses discipline differences, definitions of 'publication', versioning problems, digital preservation, costing and funding models, and metadata standards. The resolution of these issues will be important for the future of self-archiving.

Part 4
Models and economics of scholarly publishing

This final part of the volume contains three chapters, beginning with Louise Edwards' 'Electronic books' (Chapter 8). In a sense she is saying, 'Wait a minute, in all this discussion of the minutiae of scholarly publications we forget that we are still talking about the book, which has been with us for centuries, and will continue to evolve under the influence of major technological innovations.' This is indeed a timely reminder, for the debate on scholarly publishing and access seems to centre principally on the individual article or journal rather than the book, yet the book remains with us as powerfully as ever. This is because the book performs a critical cultural, educational and social role, and there is every likelihood that this role will continue as the e-book takes root. Therefore, Edwards' chapter presents an overview of where technology might take us in our relationship to the book, and what the new 'model' for the book might encompass.

Dr John Houghton's chapter, 'Economics of publishing and the future of scholarly communication', is much less speculative and deals quite rigorously with an analysis of the economics of scientific and professional publishing. He maintains that the underlying economic characteristics of information in print and online forms go a considerable way towards explaining the recent evolution of the scholarly communication system, the emergence of the so-called crisis in scholarly communication and such recent developments as the Big Deal subscription model for access to online journals. Houghton argues that digitization and online access and distribution fundamentally change the underlying economic characteristics of content products, and that these changes will affect existing business models, cost and industry structures. At the same time, research practices are changing, bringing new communication and dissemination needs. Together, these forces are changing scholarly communication and scientific publishing in ways that are yet to become entirely clear.

Finally, in Chapter 10 Dr Peter Shepherd (Project COUNTER) addresses the thorny issue of 'Usage statistics – achieving credibility, consistency and compatibility'. This topic is significant in evaluating the use of scholarly materials, and determining whether these materials are cost-effective. However, until recently the absence of a widely accepted international standard for the measurement of online usage of publications made it difficult to evaluate the relative usage of different titles. To address this problem COUNTER has developed an international code of practice governing the recording and exchange of vendor-generated online usage data. Shepherd's chapter discusses the COUNTER Code of Practice, focusing on journals and databases; it was published in January 2003 and has since been widely adopted by publishers.

Thoughtful readers will notice that some topics are not covered, most notably copyright. This is because copyright varies enough from country to country for almost any chapter on the topic to seem rather parochial, and because no expert on international copyright issues would commit to a chapter for the *International Yearbook*. In fact, this issue is so complex and so significant for the information industry that it warrants a yearbook of its own, which is on the list of future topics. This omission aside, *IYLIM 2004–2005* offers a range of perspectives on a selection of significant topics in the field of scholarly publishing, which go a considerable way towards achieving the *International Yearbook*'s aim of bringing readers up to date with developments and suggesting possible future directions in scholarly publishing for the 21st century.

The production team

The Editorial Advisory Board deserves its usual kudos for working assiduously in locating possible authors and for assessing completed chapters; they have borne a greater burden this year as the incomplete review of the Board has resulted in fewer members, with new appointments not yet made. This will be rectified in time for the next *International Yearbook*. I also extend thanks to the production team at Facet Publishing for their patience and efficiency – different faces in part, but the same high quality. Jackie Bell in Wellington has been coaxed out of 'retirement' to deal with final tidying up of the text, and for this I am especially grateful. Finally, a special thanks to this year's Associate Editor, Dr Fytton Rowland, whose expertise in scholarly publishing has been especially valuable in coaxing authors into the fold.

G. E. Gorman
Victoria University of Wellington

Part 1

OVERVIEW OF SCHOLARLY PUBLISHING IN THE 21ST CENTURY

1

Where is scholarly publishing going?

Fytton Rowland

Introduction

Scholarly publication has a very long history and until recently has experienced rather little change – as a one-time biochemist I used to say that it was 'strongly conserved during evolution', a feature that usually indicates that the function concerned is especially crucial to the survival of the organism. The organism here is the scholarly community.

It is generally observed that scholarly publishing, especially scholarly journal publishing, is a distinctive sector of the publishing industry because it exists more for the benefit of its authors than for the benefit of its readers. For a book to be published or a new magazine or newspaper to be launched, the publisher must be convinced that there will be enough readers to make the product viable. For a new scholarly journal to be launched, on the other hand, the publisher needs to be convinced that there is a sufficient community of potential authors to make it viable (Page, Campbell and Meadows, 1997).

The key functions of a scholarly journal are: to recognize the priority of the author – this person discovered this material first; to provide quality control – this work deserves to be published; to put the work on permanent record; and to disseminate the information. The whole process is overseen by peer review, whereby papers are judged for their quality before publication by two or three referees who are experts in the subject of the paper. The four functions are not usually placed in this order, and librarians will tend perhaps to put them in precisely the reverse order, but most authors are in no doubt that my order is theirs (Meadows, 1974). In particular, in recent years the development of faster means of communication has led to full journal publication losing much of its current dissemination role. Rapid short communication journals, preprint distribution and conference presentations ensure that the general gist of a person's research is well known to their scholarly community long before the full article appears (Meadows, 1998).

Technological factors driving change

Conversion of scientific publications to electronic form began with abstracts and indexes (A&I) journals in the 1960s. Initially the conversion was undertaken to facilitate the sorting operation that is needed to alphabetize the indexes of these large publications. Slightly later, the adoption of computer typesetting provided the text of the abstracts in machine-readable form as well. Development of large fixed disks and of packet-switching technology by telecommunications utilities facilitated the first online, real-time information services based on these A&I databases in the mid-1970s. Not surprisingly some scholars conceived of converting the primary, full-text literature to electronic form as well, but the available infrastructure of hardware, software and networks was inadequate to the task until the late 1980s.

Until the 1980s scholarly journals were usually typeset by firms specializing in technical setting and were still printed, in some cases, by hot metal processes. Material came in from authors as typescripts, which had to be sent to and from referees by post, and to and from typesetters and printers by van. Until the end of the 1980s, publishers did not in general have access to any machine-readable form of the texts, although by then many authors were in fact composing them on word processors. Publisher began to accept authors' keystrokes and, after editing, passing them on to typesetters. The transfer to computer typesetting meant that electronic files of the data existed – albeit often in mutually incompatible typesetting formats – and thus in principle an electronic version of an established print journal could be produced.

The development of the internet from the late 1980s onwards and especially of the world wide web from about 1992 has provided the necessary technological capability for electronic publication of full text to be practicable: widespread availability of networked PCs among prospective users; de facto standardization on Microsoft Windows; a robust network of good bandwidth and speed; and a user-friendly interface that does not require a high degree of computer knowledge among users. Beginning in about 1989, certain enthusiastic academics began to launch new, online-only journals, which they distributed free of charge. Initially the technology used was an e-mail discussion list to distribute tables of content to users, who could then download the full text of any article that interested them using anonymous file transfer protocol (FTP). This did, however, require a certain amount of IT expertise. Gopher made things easier, enabling users to reach the required files via a hierarchy of menus. But the world wide web software was the real catalyst for rapid growth, with its user-friendly graphical interface, hypertext linking, and ability to handle graphics and other non-text files. In the early 1990s the number of new electronic journals grew rapidly, although it was still much smaller than the total (over 20,000) of established print journals. An organization named the International Consortium for the Advancement of Academic Publication (ICAAP www.icaap.org/) links these journals together.

Commercial factors driving change

Two books have appeared that chart the history of scholarly publishing during the 20th century (Frederickson, 2001; Abel and Newlin, 2002). Prior to World War 2, scholarly publishing had been mostly in the hands of university presses and learned societies, who did not seek to make profits from it. Typically, societies supplied copies of their journals to members for 'free' – that is to say, the subscription to the journal was included with the membership subscription to the society. Non-member subscriptions consisted of sales to libraries and other institutions. This model persists in small societies. Larger societies and university presses still publish a significant proportion of scholarly journals, and often charge a lower subscription to personal subscribers (members in the case of societies) than to institutions. Certain long-established journals, however, have always been published by commercial publishers, for example *Nature* (Macmillan) and *Philosophical Magazine* (Taylor & Francis).

After World War 2 there was a great expansion of higher education and scientific research, especially in the developed countries of Europe and North America, resulting in a greater quantity of research data needing to be published. The commercial sector of the publishing industry moved in to fill this need, with Robert Maxwell's Pergamon Press in the forefront. A major attraction to publishing companies of this sector of the publishing business was cashflow. Journals are bought on annual advance subscription, meaning that the publishers receive most of their income before the start of the year, while expenses are incurred gradually through the year – an unusual example of a positive cashflow business.

In addition to those journals operated entirely by businesses, some society journals came to be published by separate publishers under various forms of agreement with the societies (Singleton, 1980): Blackwell's, for example, has always had a high proportion of society journals in its portfolio. Over time, the proportion of commercially published journals has risen, due in great measure to the launching of new titles to cover new or expanding fields of research.

For a variety of reasons, commercially published journals tend to have higher prices (measured in price per page or price per 1000 words) than those from not-for-profit organizations. The need for the former to generate profit for their shareholders is one of these reasons, but possibly not the most significant. More important is the fact that the commercial journals are generally newer and more specialized, and thus have lower circulations than the not-for-profit ones; their 'first-copy costs' have to be spread over fewer sales. Furthermore, in general for many years journals have been rising in price more rapidly than general price inflation, outstripping the budgets of libraries, and leading to the perceived 'journals crisis'. Libraries have had to cancel subscriptions year after year and have thus been less and less able to maintain comprehensive collections, even in their institutions' chief research areas. Often they have robbed the book budget to maintain the journal collection, to the annoyance of their users in those fields where book publication remains dominant.

There was optimism among librarians that electronic publication could lead to a fall in journal prices as the costs of print were eliminated.

Developments after 1994

In the mid-1990s the stage was thus set for the scholarly journal literature to move to electronic publication on a large scale. Various studies, notably one undertaken for the European Union in 1992, suggested that by 2000 the proportion of all literature that was delivered electronically would be substantial – perhaps 25% – and that the science, technology and medicine (STM) journal literature would be in the vanguard of this development (Laukamm, 1993). Major scholarly publishers were cautious, however, as they found it difficult to predict a business model that would protect their revenue base. First-copy costs are a high proportion of total costs for low-circulation publications, and the revenue from library subscriptions had always provided assurance that this would be covered. Furthermore, the publishing industry has traditionally not invested heavily in capital equipment – in most cases printing was contracted out – but the transfer to electronic publishing was clearly going to necessitate heavy investment in hardware, software and staff training, for an uncertain return.

Nevertheless, beginning from the 1995 subscription year for the early adopters, and from 1996 for a larger number, publishers began to offer electronic access to their titles to their institutional subscribers. The typical business model was to offer print plus electronic access as a package, either at the same price as print-only, or at a modest premium (for instance 10%). In the latter case, print-only might or might not still be offered as an alternative; if it was not offered, some customers objected to paying a premium for an electronic product that they did not want. Electronic-only was occasionally offered, too, perhaps at a 10% discount from the print-only price, but few libraries dared to switch immediately to an untried product. Libraries began to include e-journal lists on their websites, often putting the publishers' free-with-print offerings into the list along with the early 1990s new free journals.

These business models did not, however, help libraries with the journals crisis at all, as prices continued to rise. Furthermore, within the commercial sector of the scholarly publishing industry many mergers and takeovers have taken place, leading to an increasingly concentrated industry. The investment needed to transfer effectively to electronic publication may have been a contributing factor to this trend. Certainly, the smaller publishers in the not-for-profit sector found difficulty in coping with the technological changes involved, and some received assistance from university-based projects such as HighWire Press (Stanford) and Project Muse (Johns Hopkins). Others used the services of intermediaries such as OCLC in the USA or Ingenta in the UK to make their electronic journals available. Another body that provides useful advice and assistance to smaller publishers is the Association of Learned and Professional Society Publishers (ALPSP), based in the UK but with an increasingly international membership; ALPSP has commissioned several major surveys of authors, of which ALPSP (2002) is the most recent. The early period of the conversion to electronic publishing was documented in an influential book edited by Peek and Newby (1996), and the authoritative work of Tenopir and King (2000) provides voluminous data covering the period of transition.

Consortia and the Big Deal

In this new situation of the late 1990s both libraries and publishers adopted new approaches. Libraries, realizing that they were fragmented compared with the increasingly concentrated publishers, began to band together in consortia to negotiate with publishers on a more equal basis of size. Some of these consortia were organized by governments at national or provincial levels, while others were organized by librarians themselves. The deals that they were able to negotiate also varied, but typically publishers required that their total income from the members of a consortium should be similar to their previous revenue from those customers, but far wider access to the electronic resources was provided. The distribution of the overall bill from a publisher between the various members of the consortium might be a matter for internal negotiation within the consortium. Such deals might provide considerably better value for money, especially to the smaller institutions within a consortium, who might get access to all of a publisher's output in electronic form for the same price as was previously paid for a small number of print titles. Different consortia negotiated different deals, so the concept of a firm price for any given product began to disappear. In terms of what libraries might do with the services that they purchase, dependence on copyright law and the concept of 'fair use' or 'fair dealing' began to be supplemented, if not replaced, by a reliance on contract law and the terms of licences. These too were negotiable, and the more powerful and better organized consortia could receive more favourable terms and conditions than other customers. An international organization, the International Coalition of Library Consortia (ICOLC, www.library.yale.edu/consortia/) now links the consortia.

Even in the absence of a consortium, publishers began to offer new kinds of tariff. While the concept of a subscription to one individual journal is unlikely to disappear completely in the near future – since some subscribers may only need a few titles – the Big Deals similar to those negotiated with consortia began to be offered to all customers. Elsevier is the largest scholarly publisher, having taken over many others in the last 15 years, including Maxwell's Pergamon Press, and their Science Direct is the biggest of the Big Deals. Under a Big Deal, a library commits itself to subscribe for a multi-year period, with a price escalator between the years and very limited scope for individual title cancellations, and can then access the whole of that publisher's stable of journals electronically. In the early years of such deals the price paid usually depended on the amount spent by that library on print journals previously. As the years go by, however, this basis becomes less and less defensible: why should the price I pay for an electronic collection in 2010 depend on what I paid for print journals 15 years earlier? Thus publishers have been seeking an alternative basis, and so far the most widely adopted one is the size of the institution, larger ones paying more and smaller ones less. Usually some sort of 'banding' approach is used, with perhaps four size bands. Even then, there are issues regarding what should be counted. If a publisher produces predominantly biomedical titles, should the bands be based on numbers of medical students rather than total numbers of students? What about postgraduate-only institutions, likely to be small, but with a much higher intensity of use of research literature than an undergraduate institution? Banding may be only an intermediate solution.

Usage statistics and smaller deals

A more appropriate longer-term basis for charging might be one based on actual usage. One approach is simply to go to 'pay-per-view', in which every time a member of an institution accesses an article from a particular publisher, the institution is charged a small fixed fee. Although some publishers offer pay-per-view as an option for occasional purchasers, this as the sole business model is seen as inappropriate by both publishers and libraries. From the publishers' perspective, it does not bring them in the favourable cashflow that is such a big part of the advantage of the periodicals business. Nor does it bring a predictable revenue, necessary for covering their large first-copy costs. From the libraries' point of view, it does not lead to predictable costs that can be budgeted for. Hence some kind of subscription basis is still favoured by both sides.

However, a system based on the previous year's usage has attraction. A library would pay an annual subscription in advance, but the size of the subscription depends on how much use members of the institution had made of that publisher's materials in the prior year. Such a basis demands reliable usage statistics, collected consistently between publishers and between libraries, and seen by both sides to be accurate and fair. An international group, containing both publishers and librarians, has devised such a system known as COUNTER (www.projectcounter.org/), and publishers who apply COUNTER's standards may now claim to be COUNTER-compliant, opening up the possibility of usage-based subscriptions in the future (Shepherd, 2003). Incidentally a rather odd consequence of the basing of charges on the previous year's usage might be that libraries discourage users from using the electronic resources that they have paid for, since increasing use would lead to higher prices in the future!

Meanwhile, after several years' experience the Big Deal is beginning to fall from favour (Rowse, 2003). Most publishers have stables of journals that cross many disciplines, and comprehensive coverage of a discipline usually requires journals from a number of publishers. A package deal of all the titles from any one publisher is thus not a very attractive proposition to many libraries, as it will bring them many titles they do not need and fail to deliver ones that they do need. The price-escalator clause in a typical Big Deal agreement means that the deals with a few large publishers consume an increasing proportion of the total acquisitions budget as the years go by. If budget cuts occur, cancellations are concentrated on titles outside the big deals. These are likely to be titles from small, not-for-profit publishers, which are often seen to offer better value for money than the commercial titles, and may be the journals particularly favoured by the library's users. Other things being equal, the Big Deals are likely to intensify the oligopoly of the scholarly publishing industry, not necessarily something that libraries and their clients wish to see. Library consortia are therefore beginning to demand smaller package deals, often discipline-based, to buy (for example) all of Elsevier's biomedical titles, rather than all of Elsevier's titles right across the board. Publishers are now starting to offer such alternatives. So their tariff structures become ever more complex; in place of a simple annual subscription price for each individual title, a whole range of different packages are now on offer, and prices are not fixed since consortia negotiate them.

Radical alternatives: open access

The failure of electronic publication to lead to lower prices caused much disappointment in the library world, and some librarians, academics and university administrators began to think about more radical reforms to the scholarly communication system that the internet might facilitate (Harnad, 2001; Walker, 2002; Friend, 2004). Some impetus came from the new, free, electronic-only journals that started in the early 1990s; it is acknowledged, however, that this model depends on much commitment of volunteer effort by the academic editor, and on covert subsidy from the editor's employer institution in the form office space, servers, network use and so on. The model is not scalable – it might work for a journal receiving 100 submissions per annum, but cannot work for one receiving 10,000, which inevitably needs significant numbers of staff. Nor is it stable; if the founder editor moves on, retires or dies there is no guarantee that the archive of published material from that journal will continue to be available. This is unacceptable given that permanent archiving is one of the four key functions of a scholarly journal. However, these experiences led a group of enthusiasts to continue to work on concepts for a scholarly communication system that would cost less than the current one, and be under more direct control of the academic communities themselves.

The idea of an electronic journal available without charge to readers everywhere is an attractive one, in accord with the traditional ethics of scholarship, which see all scholars within a given discipline as colleagues working together to increase the sum of human knowledge. It also seems to many people a morally desirable objective that scholars in poor countries should have access to the published literature; this they often been denied in the past, and present-day initiatives such as HINARI, INASP, AGORA and EIFL all seek to remedy this situation.

If journals are to be made available at no charge to readers, however, some source of funding is required to cover their unavoidable costs. Although various ideas have been floated, opinion seems to be homing in on the concept of a publication charge levied on each paper accepted for publication, to cover the costs of its refereeing and editing, mounting it on a server and the future maintenance of the archive. This charge would be paid by the funding body that sponsored the research reported in the paper, or by the institution that employs the author (Lamb, 2004). A number of journals based on these principles have been launched, some by established publishers (for example the Institute of Physics with *New Journal of Physics*) and some by new companies such as BioMed Central. No established journals have been converted to open access completely as yet. But the prestigious journal *Proceedings of the National Academy of Sciences (PNAS)* in the USA has recently announced that if authors pay a publication charge their papers will be made freely available immediately. The assumption here is that, as the number of authors paying the charge rises, the library subscription price can fall, leading to a gradual conversion to open access.

The future for not-for-profit publishers

Not-for-profit publishers use the surpluses generated by their journal publishing operations to cross-subsidize other activities. University presses, for example, may use surpluses on journals to help pay for the publication of academic books, especially in the humanities, that are in themselves not viable projects. Learned society publishers may use the journal surplus to help pay for regional or specialized subject groups that are in themselves too small to pay their way. Many other society activities are inherently non-revenue earning – for example, efforts to lobby governments on behalf of their subject field – and the publishing surplus helps to cover these expenses, thus keeping membership subscriptions down.

Thus for societies, in particular, there is a potential internal conflict. On the one hand, members as readers probably want the widest possible access to the scholarly literature, and as authors want their own papers to have visibility and impact. On the other hand, the society as a whole wants good revenues so that all of its important activities can continue. Some of the larger society publishers have in the last few years been among the most hawkish of publishers in opposing open access.

It was noted earlier that the Big Deals potentially threaten smaller, mainly not-for-profit, publishers by consuming too large a share of libraries' acquisitions budgets. However, electronic publication itself, and especially its open access variant, may also present problems for these smaller organizations. Small societies have low costs because much of their effort is provided voluntarily by members, and they do not carry a large superstructure of senior management. Often the subscription to the journal is combined with the membership subscription and members receive personal copies of the printed journal. Many of these members no doubt work in institutions that themselves hold non-member subscriptions to the same journal. If dual (print and electronic) publishing is instituted, members of the institution are entitled to free access to the electronic version through their institutional library. Some of them may decide to cancel their membership of the society, if the journal was their only real benefit from belonging. Now suppose that the journal become open access. Now all of the members of the society can receive the journal free of charge electronically. Even more may cancel their membership, and potentially the society may go into terminal decline, and eventually cease to be able to publish their journal at all (Rowland, 2004).

Societies, especially the smaller ones, are presented with an urgent problem. Many do not dare experiment with open access. The alternative of charging a subscription but making access free to all papers after six months or one year is a compromise solution that some are using.

Radical alternatives: the subversive proposal

In certain disciplines, notably physics, there had long been a tradition of preprint exchange – researchers sent copies of their papers before publication to colleagues and friends around the world. In print days there had been abortive attempts to systematize this practice, such as the Smithsonian Information Exchange. In 1991, however, Paul Ginsparg at the Los Alamos Laboratory in the USA established an electronic preprint exchange in high energy physics, which has operated successfully ever since, though recently it has migrated with Ginsparg to Cornell University. It covers all areas of physics, and also mathematics, nonlinear sciences, computer science and quantitative biology. It also now includes postprints (published articles) as well as preprints. Similar services exist for psychology (Cogprints) and economics (RepEc), but it is in physics that the concept has achieved the widest acceptance. The major publishers of physics journals have not opposed the development and it does not seem to have hurt their businesses.

Impatient at the slow progress towards free availability of electronic scholarly articles, some scholars made what they termed a 'subversive proposal' (Okerson and McDonnell, 1995; Harnad, 2001). They suggested that authors should simply mount their own papers on their own websites, available free of charge to all, in both pre- and post-publication forms. Thus even if a publisher charges a high price for electronic access to their journals, those papers can still be obtained free from their authors. In many cases this activity is technically illegal, since authors usually agree to transfer copyright to the journal when they submit their papers for publication. At first, some journals stated that they would not consider for publication any papers that already had been made freely available as electronic preprints – the Inglefinger rule – because they deemed them to be already published. However, views have mellowed and many publishers do now allow the mounting of preprints, postprints or both on the authors' servers (Gadd, Oppenheim and Probets, 2003). Elsevier has recently joined the group of publishers that allows both.

However, a purely personal server may not remain in existence in the long term, and may not be very visible to world wide web search engines. Recently these issues have been addressed. The Open Archives Initiative (OAI, www.openarchives.org/) provides technical standards to render distributed servers visible to service providers, so that a user can search all OAI-compliant servers seamlessly in a single search. And a movement has gained momentum for each institution to have an OAI-compliant server carrying an Institutional Repository, where all research outputs produced by members of that institution can be mounted. Such a server might carry types of material other than research articles from that university as well, but so far as research publications are concerned an OAI-compliant institutional repository would in principle provide free access worldwide to research results from that university. This would potentially increase the visibility and impact of work done at that institution.

Radical alternatives: deconstructed journals

Several commentators have discussed concepts such as the deconstructed journal, the virtual journal and the overlay journal. The common theme behind these models is that the actual location of the accessible electronic full text of a paper is now irrelevant. The important points are that it should be possible for readers to find it and download it, and that a seal of quality approval should be applied by reputable experts in the paper's field. In principle, the archival storage of a paper could be the responsibility of one organization while provision of access to it could be the responsibility of another, and the original peer review could have been conducted by a third. Funding for each of these functions would have to be assured. If large distributed repositories exist, a 'journal' in a specialized subject field might simply consist of an overlay on the repository. Readers could even specify personal journals reflecting their own interests. One paper might be in several 'virtual journals' if it fell within more than one subject field. It is too early to say whether this kind of model will find favour in the future; perhaps the 'brand name' associated with publication in a particular journal (effectively, a particular editor and editorial board) will retain too strong an attraction (Smith, 1999).

Peer review and quality control

Since the advent of the internet, it has been suggested from time to time that peer review by refereeing may no longer be needed, since some people feel that this is a form of 'rationing' that was necessary for print but is unnecessary given the virtually limitless capacity of the world wide web. A more radical view even sees it as censorship. A more reformist view suggests that peer review by just two or three experts might be replaced by a more open and democratic type of reviewing in which readers in general are invited to comment on submitted papers before they are finalized and declared 'published'. Still less radically, others have implemented a normal form of peer review followed by publication, but with open peer commentary after the event – comments from readers and perhaps rejoinders from the original authors being appended to the published paper.

Since one of the key functions of scholarly literature is the quality control provided by peer review, most scholars would resist its complete abolition. Already there is too much to read; the quality assurance offered by the well known 'brand names' of leading journals is a valuable time saver for readers, and also provides the mechanism by which the quality of performance of academics and research workers can be judged. However, some change in the process is likely, and perhaps more journals will move to open peer review or at least open peer commentary. There is an unanswered question regarding the status of papers that are changed from their original form as a consequence of peer commentary: a peer-reviewed paper has historically been regarded as a static entity so that readers can be confident that what they see is what the referees approved. Mechanisms are needed to ensure that interactivity, which is a virtue of electronic communication, does not lead to a decline in the perceived quality of scholarly papers. A very thorough review of the literature about peer review has been published by Weller (2001).

It is also generally agreed that on any institutional or discipline-based repository each paper must be clearly labelled to distinguish between preprints (not yet refereed and published) and postprints (already published in a refereed journal), in order to maintain the necessary quality control.

Conclusion

The issues addressed above are discussed in greater depth in later chapters. As of this writing, the major issues for scholarly publishing in the immediate future are as follows:

1 Will open access *publishing* (the Gold Route) expand substantially, either by the launch of more new journals or, perhaps more importantly, through the conversion of existing established titles? Can this be achieved by gradualism, such as is being tried by *PNAS*? Is it sufficient for articles to be available free of charge only after a time lag?

2 Will open access achieved by self-archiving (the Green Route) flourish? It is necessary not only for institutions to establish institutional repositories, but also for academic authors to populate those repositories with their articles. How will they be persuaded to do so?

3 If institutional repositories really take off, what will be the effect on publishers' sales? Will libraries cancel subscriptions on the grounds that most of the articles are freely available? Will publishers' attitudes to self-archiving harden again if this happens? Or will they instead decide to make their journals open access publications themselves?

4 How will learned societies – large and small – survive if open access comes to predominate? Does it matter if they do not?

5 Will the 'journal' as an identifiable entity survive at all? What are the prospects for the deconstructed journal, the virtual journal, the overlay journal?

References

Abel, R. E. and Newlin, L. W. (eds) (2002) *Scholarly Publishing: books, journals publishers, and libraries in the twentieth century*, New York, John Wiley & Sons.

Association of Learned and Professional Society Publishers (2002) *Authors and Electronic Publishing: the ALPSP research study on authors' and readers' views of electronic research communication*, Worthing, ALPSP.

Frederickson, E. H. (ed.) (2001) *A Century of Scientific Publishing*, Amsterdam, IOS Publishing.

Friend, F. J. (2004) How Can There Be Open Access to Journal Articles?, *Serials*, **17** (1), 37–40.

Gadd, E., Oppenheim, C. and Probets, S. (2003) RoMEO Studies 4: an analysis of publishers' copyright agreements, *Learned Publishing*, **16** (4), 293–308.

Harnad, S. (2001) The Self-Archiving Initiative, *Nature*, **410**, 1024–5. Other papers by Stevan Harnad are listed at www.ecs.soton.ac.uk/~harnad/intpub.html [accessed 28 June 2004]

Lamb, C. (2004) Open Access Publishing Models: opportunity or threat to scholarly and academic publishers?, *Learned Publishing*, **17** (2), 143–50.

Laukamm, T. (1993) *Strategic Study on New Opportunities for Publishers in the Information Services Market*, Luxembourg, European Commission, report no. 14926 EN, A13–14.

Meadows, A. J. (1974) *Communication in Science*, London, Butterworths.

Meadows, A. J. (1998) *Communicating Research*, San Diego, Academic Press.

Okerson, A. S and McDonnell, J. J. (1995) *Scholarly Journals at the Crossroads: a subversive proposal for scholarly publishing*, Washington, Association of Research Libraries.

Page, G., Campbell, R. and Meadows, A. J. (1997) *Journal Publishing*, Cambridge UK, Cambridge University Press.

Peek, R. P. and Newby, G. B. (eds) (1996) *Scholarly Publishing: the electronic frontier*, Cambridge MA, The MIT Press.

Rowse, M. (2003) Information Industry Developments, *Serials*, **16** (2), 159–62.

Rowland, F. (2004) Scholarly Journal Publishing in New Zealand, *Learned Publishing*, in press.

Shepherd, P. T. (2003) COUNTER: from conception to compliance, *Learned Publishing*, **16** (3), 201–5.

Singleton, A. (1980) *Learned Societies Journals and Collaboration with Publishers*, Leicester, Primary Communication Research Centre.

Smith, J. W. T. (1999) The Deconstructed Journal: a new model for academic publishing, *Learned Publishing*, **12** (2), 79–92.

Tenopir, C. and King, D. W. (2000) *Towards Electronic Journals: realities for scientists, librarians and publishers*, Washington, SLA Publishing.

Walker, T. J. (2002) Two Societies Show How to Profit by Providing Free Access, *Learned Publishing*, **15** (4), 279–84.

Weller, A. C. (2001) Editorial Peer Review: its strengths and weaknesses, Silver Spring MD, American Society for Information Science and Technology.

2

Collaborative transformations in scholarly publishing

Alicia Wise

Introduction

Contributions to this *International Yearbook* are intended for the reflective practitioner in library science and information management. There will be few of you who are not intimately familiar with the raging debate on open access publishing models. Other chapters will provide future readers with all the background they might wish about the current state of this debate. I would like to begin by offering you a personal perspective on this.

The polarization of scholarly publishing discussions into 'pro' and 'anti' open access models has made for good press: raising our collective profile with academic leaders, funding agencies, and governments. It has also over-simplified most of the issues in the process.

I have a strong sense of *déjà vu* in all of this, and it stems from the time way back in the mid-1990s when I was still an archaeologist. The media had long been interested in archaeology, but that period saw the introduction of engaging television productions targeted at the interested home viewer. So far, so good. Many archaeologists were delighted that their friends and family finally understood what they did for a sort of living. There was a negative side, too. Those programmes left 'the public' with the idea that archaeologists could uncover huge buried cities in three short days without mussing their garish jumpers or slowing down for a cup of tea. Viewers didn't appreciate, in fact were never really told about, the many hours of toil that had to take place for every hour of glamorous digging. The fund-raising, laboratory analysis, training, teaching, planning, and countless hours spent writing scholarly articles never really seemed interesting enough to broadcast. This brings us nicely back to where we started.

Librarians and publishers both benefit from the higher profile of the information professions as a result of the scholarly communication debate, but we seem to be at considerable risk of being written off as finger-pointing whiners who cannot organize ourselves out of a tricky position. Digital technologies are disruptive, enabling radical new approaches to managing and using information. As a result the information creation and supply chain is transforming before our eyes, and it is not always comfortable to be somewhere in the middle. It seems to me that librarians and publishers have more in common with one another, and more to gain from collaboratively addressing shared challenges, than from attempting to do one another out of existence. You would probably expect such a perspective from someone who recently moved from a funding agency in the academic sector to a collective licensing society for publishing, but it is heartfelt.

A shared challenge

Where are librarians and publishers going together? In future – maybe ten years from now, maybe longer – information will be similar to electricity or water and basically accessible on tap wherever we are, whenever we need it (at least in the 'developed' world). By information I mean both serious, scholarly stuff and entertaining fluff – in fact, it should be increasingly difficult to distinguish between these. Information will be available in a personalized way. Perhaps we'll even wake up in the morning to discover a perfect cup of coffee waiting, and all the information that will be helpful to us on that day.

What will it take to get there? Coherence across all information types, from creation through management to use. It is very important to emphasize that this is not simply about published books and journals – that may well be the easy bit. Coherence of experience for the information user requires easy, global, personalized access to analysis, data, expertise, games, hypotheses, images, maps, quizzes, records, sound, synthesis, text and any other kind of informative stuff that can be imagined.

Librarians and publishers are very good at managing text, even if we do not always like the prices charged for aspects of this management. Both groups increasingly work with images and data. At the leading edge in both communities there is a broader range of activities – for example, librarians are gaining increased opportunity to create and manage learning objects, and chemistry publishers are integrating complex three-dimensional protein structures. But even at the leading edge no organizations currently appear to be working with all lifecycle stages of the full spectrum of required materials. That's beyond the 'bleeding' edge at present, but will certainly change.

Meeting the coherence challenge probably requires that definitions of 'librarian' and 'publisher' transform. I predict that both professions will be much more service-orientated than content-focused in future. By this I mean that we will define our primary roles not as managing a list, imprint or collection but rather as supporting learning, research and living.

Coherence requires that we solve a series of complex, but essentially technical, problems that continue to stump us: business models, copyright, distributed processing, semantic compatibility, system interoperability, metadata, personalization, visualization, portal development, preservation, quality assurance, training and many others. None of these issues is too hard for us to solve as a species, but perhaps they are too hard for us to solve only from within the information profession. It is more likely to become essential that we work with a wide variety of professionals with varying skill sets, approaches, and vocabularies. Librarians and publishers working together will have between them a wealth of experience in dealing with multimedia content and a wide spectrum of creators and users, and will be particularly expert in dealing with text. A shared challenge will be to convince other experts that lessons we have learned over hundreds of years are widely applicable to 'their' areas and 'their' problems. We will need to listen to those others as well, because they also have expertise and wisdom to share. Listening is likely to be more difficult than telling. Whatever happens, it should be an incredibly stimulating and empowering future that we shape.

Copy rights and moral rights

Widely identified as a major barrier to providing access, and much mis-understood, copyright was largely invented to ensure that authors, artists and others could scrape out a meagre existence from the fruits of their creative labours (for good introductions see Alikhan and Mashelkar, 2003; Jones and Benson, 2002; or World Intellectual Property Organization, n.d.).

Moral rights are often collated under the term copyright or under the broader heading of intellectual property rights, and are perhaps not as well understood in the English-speaking world as in the French-speaking world (Holderness, 1998). There are different moral rights in different countries, but broadly creators have moral rights to be identified as the creator of a work, and to prevent derogatory treatment of their works. Unlike copy-right, moral rights are about exercising control of presentation and use rather than about remuneration. In academia we place a great deal of weight on proper citation of sources, and spend time and energy detect-ing plagiarism and preventing it (for example, the Joint Information Systems Committee Plagiarism Advisory Service online at http://online. northumbria.ac.uk/faculties/art/information_studies/Imri/Jiscpas/site/ jiscpas.asp). Proper citation reflects an author's moral right to paternity. The other moral rights tend to be overlooked in academic circles.

There are a number of intellectual property challenges facing librari-ans and publishers, including the following:

- Now that digital technologies allow rapid, inexpensive copying, does copyright remain a valid and enabling framework for ensuring fair remuneration? The fascinating debates between copyright advocates and the emerging 'copy left' will hopefully shed light as well as heat on this topic (Lessig, 2004; Picciotto and Campbell, 2003).
- Can administrators, authors, funders, librarians and publishers come to agreement about fair and balanced approaches to managing intellectual

property? The work of the Zwolle Group is notable here (2004).

- Will digital rights management (DRM) technologies evolve to provide a transparent infrastructure for the web? These content packaging solutions developed by the creative industries are often perceived as too tightly controlling access to and use of copyright material (for good introductions see Bide, 2004; Mitchell, 2004; Renaud, 2003). Alternative approaches include the development of reputation-based and trust-based networks (such as eBay).

All the stakeholders in intellectual property exchanges need to engage in debate about these and other challenges. Neither librarians nor publishers have interests that are 100% aligned with those of authors and other creators. For this reason engagement with creator representatives (for example unions and collecting societies) is likely to be essential to both.

Communities in partnership
E-science

A particularly powerful example of positive collaboration between otherwise colliding worlds comes from the intersection of computer science and the natural sciences. This marriage has led to the birth of a movement variously called 'e-science', 'the grid', 'grids', or 'cyber-infrastructure' (Atkins et al., 2003; Berman, Fox and Hey, 2003). Some of these developments are beginning to be applied to library-type content (see www.internet2.edu/initiatives/ and www.dcc.ac.uk/).

E-learning

There is also growing awareness about the development work needed to overcome pedagogic, technologic and organizational challenges and bring the e-learning and digital library communities closer together (Lynch and McLean, 2004; Brophy, Markland and Jones, 2003). The customization of, and interoperability between, course management systems and digital content resources is immature. Access management is not handled in the same way by the two educational communities, much less commercial suppliers, and this is particularly challenging in the face of great demand for personalized learning experiences. It is perhaps unsurprising that bringing these communities together is so very promising, and so very challenging at this time of great change and innovation, stimulated by new technologies in both.

E-commerce

A third important community with which to work in partnership is that formed by those who administer business and management information systems. In academia these systems are represented by the finance, registry and other central systems that keep the university running. Such systems could hold the key to meeting personalization challenges, but are quite rightfully secure fortresses not easily made interoperable. In the UK, follow-up to the very successful corporate information focus activity funded by the JISC (www.jisc.ac.uk/index.cfm?name=programme_corporate) includes new research into frameworks to guide campus-wide systems integration.

Weaving a tapestry

Efforts to build enterprise-wide information technology frameworks in academia are new and exciting. In the UK, for example, the JISC has established a funding stream for such frameworks because:

> Technology is becoming increasingly embedded in the systems and processes of our educational institutions. Aspects of research, learning and teaching and information management now rely upon technology to support related processes. Although technology has the potential to extend and improve educational activities, this potential can only be fully realised if the activities are built upon a stable and coherent technical infrastructure. (JISC, 2003)

The programme is also intended to bring together research and development funding in e-science, information environments, managed learning environments, middleware and network provision.

Preservation

Cracking the digital preservation conundrum is another essential task for librarians and publishers. There has been growing concern among memory organizations such as libraries about the loss of information created electronically and published online in the early days of the world wide web. For many years there has also been pressure on publishers to guarantee long-term access to their content, before libraries would consent to licensing them or even contemplate cancelling print. JSTOR and other organizations have clearly demonstrated that lack of confidence about preservation is a considerable barrier to moving to electronic-only publication (see www.jstor.org/about/need.html).

There are hopeful signs of increased awareness of this challenge by funders and legislators, and of concerted collaborative action by librarians and publishers. Good examples include the Digital Preservation Coalition in the UK (www.dpconline.org/graphics/), the e-Depot and digital preservation initiative at the National Library of the Netherlands (www.kb.nl/kb/resources/frameset_kb.html?/kb/menu/ken-arch-en.html), the JSTOR electronic archiving initiative (www.jstor.org/about/earchive.html), the Preserving Access to Digital Information initiative at the National Library of Australia (www.nla.gov.au/padi/), and the US National Digital Information Infrastructure and Preservation Program (www.digitalpreservation.gov/).

It is also welcome that a key recommendation of the recent UK Select Committee that examined open access publishing is:

> The preservation of digital material is an expensive process that poses a significant technical challenge. This Report recommends that the British Library receives sufficient funding to enable it to carry out this work. It also recommends that work on new regulations for the legal deposit of non-print publications begins immediately. Failure to take these steps would result in a substantial breach in the intellectual record of the UK.
> (Select Committee on Science and Technology, 2004)

Digital preservation is rightly recognized by the Select Committee as a particular challenge for open access publishing, whether in the form of the author pays model or e-print repositories within institutions or subject domains. Right now, to my cynical eye, it appears that a great deal of lip service is paid to this problem but that there is too much buck passing at a more practical level.

For example, in the admirable Bethesda Principles, a publication meets the criteria of being open access if users have 'a free, irrevocable, worldwide perpetual right of access' (BioMed Central, 2003). The perpetual part of this access is underpinned by a statement that

> A complete version of the work and all supplemental materials, including a copy of the permission as stated above, in a suitable standard electronic format is deposited immediately upon initial publication in at least one online repository that is supported by an academic institution, scholarly society, government agency, or other well-established organization that seeks to enable open access, unrestricted distribution, interoperability, and long-term archiving (for the biomedical sciences, PubMed Central is such a repository).   (BioMed Central, 2003)

There unfortunately does not appear to be a way to track whether this requirement is met, or whether there is long-term digital preservation expertise and a secure and stable funding stream for the repositories.

A properly managed approach, including formal accreditation of digital preservation services, is very much needed. Without this, funding for digital preservation is subject to evolving political priorities often intended for pump-priming rather than long term service provision. Hopefully this is a challenge that funding bodies and governments can together overcome, but it will take the unified voices of librarians and publishers to raise awareness of the issues at that level. It is most welcome that the British Library and other national libraries are prepared to lead in this area.

Conclusion

The broad vision outlined at the start of this paper is the reason I have chosen to move into a collective licensing society working with publishers, their partners and their customers on intellectual property rights issues. It is very satisfying to dig into one of the serious challenges – copyright – that must be sorted out. Working in my previous roles at the Joint Information Systems Committee was an incredible privilege, enabling me to have an overview of innovative IT developments across disciplines.

Many of those innovative IT projects – but not all or even most – involved librarians, publishers and other information professionals. It was frustrating at times to realize the extraordinary difficulty with which experts from different communities come to perceive themselves as having shared problems. This perception is usually a necessary precursor to active collaboration in order to overcome shared problems. Librarians and publishers could do so much to raise each others' profile that it was a little frustrating to see them so often working in opposition.

Back out here in the real world, I realize that everyone is really busy improving their contribution to the bigger picture but without knowing what that bigger picture is. There are incredible communication gaps – is this ironic in the information profession? – as well as suspicion, distrust and misunderstanding. The polarization of the open access debate is a symptom of a much deeper and more important communication and trust-building challenge.

JISC experiences also suggest that it is essential to summarize clearly what it is that one wants policy makers to do at every possible opportunity. Policy makers are generally very busy and working hard to get many many things right. For this reason, I would like to end this paper a little unusually by making some suggestions to those who might read this article, or have influence over others who will not:

Recommendations for funders

I recommend that you:

1 Commit to the long-term preservation of data and publications that you fund, and not just to providing access to these important outputs in the short term.
2 Fund the research necessary to understand what the long-term implications of such a commitment will be, and options for delivering upon it.

3 Clarify your policies on copyright and moral rights, in partnership with rights owners and users.

Recommendations for researchers in library and information science

I recommend that you:

1 Experiment actively with models for the acquisition, management, and preservation of non-textual resources.
2 Commit to inter-disciplinary research by choosing to engage actively in the e-learning, e-science and/or middleware agendas.
3 Don't be modest when you do so, as the library community has an enormous amount to contribute to inter-disciplinary work.

Recommendations for librarians and information practitioners

I recommend that you:

1 Make friends with a publisher near you today. My dictionary describes a publisher as one who 'prepares and issues, makes generally known, and announces formally'. That calling is not so far from that of a librarian.
2 Find out what research and development your new friend is doing on issues of shared interest, rather than risk reinventing wheels.
3 Experiment actively with adding non-textual resources to your collections.
4 Scope the range of services you would like to provide in ten years' time, rather than the collections you would like to provide.

Recommendations for publishers

I recommend that you:

1 Talk more about the challenges you face, especially with customers.

Share in robust ways that enable competition but prevent unnecessary duplication of effort, especially expensive research and development effort.
2 Listen to creators' voices calling for balanced approaches to copyright management. They won't be going away.

References

Alikhan, S. and Mashelkar, R. (2003) *Intellectual Property and Competitive Strategies in the 21st Century*, The Hague, Kluwer Law International.

Atkins, D. E., Droegemeier, K. K., Feldman, S. I., Garcia-Molina, H., Klein, M. L., Messerschmitt, D. E., Messina, P., Ostriker, J. P. and Wright, M. H. (2003) *Revolutionizing Science and Engineering Through Cyberinfrastructure*, National Science Foundation, www.cise.nsf.gov/sci/reports/toc.cf.

Berman, F., Fox, G. and Hey, T. (eds) (2003) *Grid Computing: making the global infrastructure a reality*, Communications Networking and Distributed Computing Series, Chichester, John Wiley.

Bide, M. (2004) Digital Rights Management: preventing or enabling access?, *Serials*, **17** (2), 141–7.

BioMed Central (2003), www.biomedcentral.com/openaccess/bethesda/#definition.

Brophy, P., Markland, M. and Jones, C. (2003) *LinkER: Linking Digital Libraries and Virtual Learning Environments: Evaluation and review final report: formative evaluation of the DiVLE Programme*, Centre for Research in Library and Information Management, www.jisc.ac.uk/uploaded_documents/Linker-d5-MASTER.doc.

Holderness, M. (1998) Moral Rights and Authors' Rights: the keys to the information age, *Journal of Information, Law and Technology*, (1), http://elj.warwick.ac.uk/jilt/infosoc/98_1hold/.

Joint Information Systems Committee (2003) JISC Framework Programme, www.jisc.ac.uk/index.cfm?name=programme_frameworks.

Jones, H. and Benson, C. (2002) *Publishing Law*, 2nd edn, London, Routledge.

Lessig, L. (2004) *Free Culture: how big media uses technology and the law to lock down culture and control creativity*, New York Penguin Press.

Lynch, C. A. and McLean, N. (2004) *Interoperability between Information and Learning Environments: bridging the gaps*, a white paper produced by the IMS

Global Learning Consortium and the Coalition for Networked Information, www.imsglobal.org/digitalrepositories/CNIandIMS_2004.pdf.

Mitchell, J. T. (2004) *DRM: the good, the bad, and the ugly*. Paper presented at the *College, Code and Copyright Symposium* sponsored by the Center for Intellectual Property in the Digital Environment, University of Maryland University College, http://interactionlaw.com/documentos/DRM_good_bad_ugly.pdf.

Picciotto, S. and Campbell, D. (2003) Whose Molecule is it Anyway? Private and Social Perspectives on Intellectual Property. In Hudson, A. (ed.), *New Perspectives on Property Law, Obligations and Restitution*, London, Cavendish, 279–303.

Renaud, A. (2003) *Bringing Down the Barriers for DRM-protected Content*, Rightscom, www.rightscom.com/Portals/0/paper_barrierstoDRMprotected%20contentAR.pdf.

Select Committee on Science and Technology (2004) *Tenth Report*, summary, www.publications.parliament.uk/pa/cm200304/cmselect/cmsctech/399/39903.htm.

World International Property Organization (n.d.) www.wipoint/about-ip/en/copyright.html.

Zwolle Group (2004) www.surf.nl/copyright/.

Part 2

INSTITUTIONAL PERSPECTIVES ON SCHOLARLY PUBLISHING

3

The library's perspective on scholarly publishing in the 21st century

Colin Steele

Introduction: historical backdrop

Libraries have traditionally been responsible for the collection and storage of publications. The library's principal role was to acquire scholarly material particularly in the form of books, serials and manuscripts. Even as late as the early 1990s it could be argued that this was still the prime focus of a university library, although the diversity of formats had clearly increased. If Thomas James, the first Librarian of the refounded Bodleian Library in 1602, had been transported from the early 17th century to a typical university library in the middle of the 20th century it would not have been an unfamiliar milieu in terms of the library's core activities.

Digital transformations?

The 21st century, however, will most likely see a transformation of the library's role, not only in the access and storage of scholarly material but also in the creation and distribution of scholarly publishing.

Libraries will need, as Lougee (2002) has commented in a report for the US Council of Library and Information Resources, to move from being passive to active players in the scholarly communication chain – to become 'diffuse agents'. Since Lougee prepared her report in 2002 the framework for such changes has deepened. For instance, the institutional repository movement has taken hold and the potential for libraries to take a more proactive role in the production, storage and dissemination of scholarly knowledge has become apparent. The definition of scholarly material has also widened to encompass significant amounts of non-textual material ranging from scientific data to statistics to email archives and websites.

Hey, Director of the UK's E-science Core Programme, has termed this a 'data deluge' (Hey and Trefethen, 2003). In documenting the requisite infrastructures required for e-science, however, Hey (2004) believes that librarians 'are in danger of missing the boat' – that they should be more involved with the curation of universities' digitized intellectual property. The wider definition of what is termed scholarly publishing is reflected in two publications issued in 2004 by the American National Science Foundation and National Academy of Sciences, respectively.

The NSF report, *Knowledge Lost in Information* (2004), outlines the new 'ubiquitous knowledge environment'. Broader access to information resources, particularly via e-science and e-learning, will result in significant 'accelerators' in the creation of scholarly knowledge. This comprehensive and forward looking report acknowledges that our current ability to generate and collect data exceeds our ability to organize, manage and effectively use it. This will be a crucial issue for all who are responsible for the institutional management of information entering and leaving universities in the 21st century.

The National Academy of Sciences colloquium on Mapping Knowledge Domains indicates that profound changes are taking place in the interdisciplinary areas of science and that the issues of charting, mining, analysing, sorting, navigating and displaying knowledge needs the interaction of several professions and new techniques of analysis retrieval and visualization (Shiffrin and Borner, 2004). The role of the library in these new areas of scholarly 'publishing' is as yet still embryonic in many universities. It is clear, however, that here also new synergies will be required in institutional frameworks involving those responsible for e-research, e-learning and administrative and information structures.

Scientific, technical and medical publishing and its impact on university libraries

The second half of the 20th century saw an explosion of scientific, technical and medical (STM) publishing with a consequent impact on libraries and the research process. The Reed Elsevier empire stands as the prime symbol of the rise of the aggregated multinational publishing houses. A JP Morgan report has indicated that for Reed Elsevier scientific and medical publishing can be encapsulated by the phrase, 'big is beautiful' (Morgan, 2003). Elsevier's gross profit margin for 2003 was 34% (net 17%), with an annual price inflation rate of 6–7.5%.

The experience of Elsevier has been paralleled by such firms as Springer, Kluwer, Thomson and Taylor and Francis and is not restricted to the science publishing field. Munroe (2004) has documented the stories of some of these publishing mergers and acquisitions that still continue apace. The integration of Springer and Kluwer in 2003 was motivated, according to their purchaser, Cinven and Candover, by a desire for future financial profit. Returns to shareholders are seen as far more important than an equitable distribution of scholarly knowledge. The UK Chartered Institute of Library and Information Professionals (CILIP, 2004) has estimated that between 1998 and 2003 the average price of an academic journal rose by 58%, while the UK retail price index rose by 11% in the same period.

It was believed at one stage that electronic access would significantly reduce the costs of STM journals. STM publishers have argued that the investment in producing electronic infrastructure platforms and related portals has required significant investment. This is undoubtedly true but it could be argued that the costs are still a relatively small percentage of the gross profits recorded by the larger multinationals annually. The cost of digitizing backsets is, however, understood.

The ALPSP report *Scholarly Publishing Practice* provides a comprehensive survey of 275 journal publishers' policy and practices in relation to online publishing (Cox and Cox, 2003). The authors conclude that many publishers are still grappling with the implications of migrating from a print to an online publishing environment but that 75% of journals surveyed are now available online and that while online pricing is still tied to the print price this will be eroded in the future.

The Big Deal

In addition to the quite significant double-digit price rises of the 1990s by the major commercial multinational publishers, the appearance of the Big Deal – aggregated packages of a publisher's, or even of combined publishers', outputs – has led to the STM access vote in libraries taking larger and larger proportions of a library's budget. This has usually been at the cost of the social sciences and humanities in general, and the monograph in particular, as will be noted briefly later in this chapter.

For some universities the advantages of the Big Deal are seen as increasing content per unit of currency spent, maximizing the delivery of content for all on campus, particularly interdisciplinary studies, and providing a wider spectrum of material. Critics have argued that these deals lock universities into forward commitments over several years, accentuating the monopolization of acquisition budgets and the consequent squeezing out of the offerings of independent serial publishers, such as learned societies.

Keller (2004) in his presentation at the Fiesole 2004 Collection Development Retreat Conference, commented on the 'distraction' that has resulted from the 'preoccupation with the journal literature of STM, 90% of which has a half life of under 12 months'. He urges librarians to turn to 'an article economy and just-in-time mentality' rather than Big Deals but this, of course, is contingent on the acceptance of this approach by academic user communities and the economics of aggregated serial offerings in the future.

Academic authors

The academic user is the key to significant change in the scholarly publishing arena. Academic authors are largely isolated from the costs of the acquisition of research knowledge, which they themselves have created. The UK ALPSP report (2002), *Authors and Electronic Publishing*, found that fewer than 1% of academics considered direct financial reward to be their primary publishing objective. What attracts authors is the ability to communicate with their peer group (33%) and career advancement (22%), which comes primarily from publication in highly regarded and, even more importantly, highly cited journals. This latter point is somewhat worrying as the Institute of Scientific Information (ISI) citation rankings are not infallible and need to be taken into account with other factors in terms of research assessment.

Mabe (2003), the Director of Academic Relations for Elsevier, indicated at the Fiesole 2003 Collection Development Retreat that the prime focus for Elsevier authors was in the following order: reputation, refereeing and quality, impact factor, production speed, role of editor and editorial board, physical quality and publishing services. In a number of instances authors did not even know the publisher of the journal they were submitting to, rather it was the title and branding of the journal that counted.

The framework of scholarly publishing

The UK House of Commons (2004) Science and Technology Committee Inquiry into Scientific Publications has reflected a diversity of views as to the publishing framework of scholarly publishing. Cox (2004) has stated in his evidence to this Inquiry that 'the market is dysfunctional as price signals do not reach the real customer' – the academic reader. The user community behaves quite differently depending on their mode of use of material – as searcher, reader or author. Depending on which activity they are engaging in, they have different perceptions of value and incentive. There is a marked reluctance to pay for material except when immediate access is required, for example for commercial or research purposes. The fact that knowledge costs have increased significantly for their university libraries or research centre is often not a matter of concern to them.

A major research study, undertaken for the Australian Government Department of Education, Science and Training (DEST), revealed that while many researchers operate within Mode 2 science frameworks, for example interdisciplinary, collaborative and team focused, their publication habits are essentially 20th century Mode 1 (Houghton, Steele and Henty, 2003). In that latter context the publication is essentially a mark of reputation, recognition and branding allied to future citations, rather than a vehicle for the scholarly communication of that research.

Many researchers have often distributed the contents of that research through electronic colleges or personal web pages well before the formal publication process. The formal process of scholarly publication and its relationship with the establishment of indicators for research excellence will not change, however, until reward systems change. Authors will not change their practice unless they believe it is in their interest to change. We therefore need to establish a coherent structure of incentives within the new modes of knowledge production.

The changing information frameworks of user populations

Within the old and the new frameworks there is a need for continual monitoring of the changing information frameworks of user populations. It is salutary to note that while billions of dollars are spent around the world on acquiring scholarly material an extremely small proportion of those budgets is spent on analysing the effective use of the material and/or the wider scholarly communication process in the digital era.

One such example of shifts in usage patterns arises from the statistics derived from the Big Deal. In these analyses, which range from America to Australia, it is salutary to see that academic usage patterns often behaved somewhat erratically when viewed from the perspective of the library. At the Australian National University, Elsevier journals in specific subject disciplines, which had been cancelled by the academics themselves as being of little value, were in fact relatively highly accessed when the Big Deal made all Elsevier journals available electronically. Some of this 'substituted use' could be attributed to wider electronic access by wider subject groupings, such as the social sciences and humanities, but other factors still remain unexplained.

While there have clearly been significant changes in electronic access delivery mechanisms, the core element of scientific publishing remains the article in roughly the same form as it appeared in the print version. Many Commonwealth countries, because of the decline of their currencies, moved to electronic only access and cancelled print in the 1990s. It is interesting that the decline of the US dollar in 2003 has led to a renewed interest in scholarly communication frameworks in the USA, which perhaps offers hope for more long-term structured change since

65% of the STM market operates in that country. Reaction from the user communities to electronic access so far has been surprisingly favourable and has led to the increased use of scholarly material either at the desktop or through information commons.

Libraries – museums or malls?

In this electronic environment there has been a decided bifurcation in access patterns to physical library buildings. Academics and research users, especially in the sciences, are increasingly accessing material at their desktops and are rarely entering the library except for non-digitized backsets of periodicals and other paper material. The latter material assumes the almost archival type of use associated with manuscript collections. To the desktop users, the physical library buildings take on the ethos of a museum, while to students it has become more of a shopping mall. Libraries have become electronic commons, social places building upon the pioneering Canadian Commons developments of the 1990s, such as at Calgary and Toronto. The pressures on students from the need to meet increasing student fees has led to the 'one-stop shop' syndrome. The library has become an educational and social forum where terminal access is often just as important as reading physical texts.

The ability for Commons facilities to remain open long after main libraries have closed, allied with coffee shops, make them resemble the big bookstore chains more than traditional libraries. In several university libraries bookshops have actually become part of the library, such as at the University of Melbourne. The future will undoubtedly see a convergence of electronic publishing between libraries and bookstores particularly through virtual learning environments and the requirement to print off electronic material through 'print on demand' facilities (PODs). Evidence from those publishers who make material available on the web for free is that they tend to sell more copies where a commercial print version can be made available. Print on demand facilities will become a boom area, not just for research monographs, but also in the area of individual course pack delivery.

Institutional repositories

In this process of change, there is a need to readdress the question of what is the role of librarians in such environments. Libraries and their part in the creation and development of institutional repositories has been a significant and also hotly debated topic in 2003 and 2004. Digital publishing technologies, linked to global networking and international interoperability protocols and metadata standards, allow for an appropriately branded institutional output to serve as an indication of a university's quality and also as an effective scholarly communication tool.

Crow has stated in his seminal SPARC paper:

> Institutional repositories – digital libraries capturing and preserving the intellectual output of a university community – provide a compelling response to two strategic issues facing academic institutions. Such repositories serve as tangible indicators of a university's quality and demonstrate the societal relevance of its research activities, thus increasing the university's visibility, status, and public value; . . . and provide a critical component in the changing structure of scholarly communication – a structure that expands access to research for the academic communities that create it.
>
> Institutional repositories, by capturing, preserving, and disseminating a university's collective intellectual capital, serve as meaningful indicators of an institution's academic quality. Under the traditional system of scholarly communication, much of the intellectual output and value of an institution's intellectual property is diffused through thousands of scholarly journals. An institutional repository concentrates the intellectual product created by a university's researchers, making it easier to demonstrate its social and financial value.   (Crow, 2002, 2, 4)

Since Crow's article, many repositories have been established globally. Ware (2004) has noted, however, that the population of repositories has been affected by cultural issues affecting scholarly take-up, such as a lack of self archiving and awareness and perceived intellectual property difficulties. Ware has cited institutional repositories as part of the digital infrastructure of the modern university, offering a set of services for the management and dissemination of digital materials created by that institution.

E-print repositories and the spin-off e-presses have taken as their philosophy the requirement to 'publicize' through a safe and trusted repository the intellectual output of a particular institution. Repositories are particularly useful for the distribution of 'grey' and 'guild' literature produced by a university, especially in the social sciences and humanities. The experience of the Australian National University E-Prints Repository, which at the time of writing had one of the more significant global institutional holdings, illustrates that increasing the volume of material in the repository increases accessibility.

The fact that an ANU staff member has been dedicated to harvesting material, both from individual websites and from subject archives, has helped increase the population of the e-print archive. In this process the library becomes an agent for the distribution of scholarly publishing in addition to being a print 'receptacle' and electronic facilitator in the acquisition of scholarly material.

The crucial issue is the population of repositories. Most technical problems have been overcome and the 'tipping points' relate to cultural and political issues. One strategy is the linking of the library, as in the University of Amsterdam with the Research Office of the university. Harnad (2003) believes all university research output should be continuously accessible. In this model every researcher should have a standardized electronic CV, continuously updated with all the Research Assessment Exercise performance indicators listed and every journal paper linked to its full-text in that university's online e-print archive.

The movement to deposit material in institutional repositories often needs one-to-one dialogue or dedicated departmental meetings to explain to researchers that depositing in their own repositories will not affect their output in traditional journals, apart from the fact that such deposits often increase global access to their publications. The process of populating repositories will no doubt be incremental and modular and will require institutional backing at local and national levels.

Within the institutional settings, Lynch sees the development of repositories:

as a new strategy that allows universities to apply serious, systematic leverage to accelerate changes taking place in scholarship and scholarly communication, both moving beyond their historic relatively passive role of supporting established publishers in modernizing scholarly publishing through the licensing of digital content, and also scaling up beyond ad-hoc alliances, partnerships, and support arrangements with a few select faculty pioneers exploring more transformative new uses of the digital medium.   (Lynch, 2003)

Holistic frameworks: copyright and peer review

It is clear that the scholarly communication environment is in a state of flux. We need to look at the whole scholarly communication process in a wider context, from the act of creation of knowledge to distribution in a holistic sense. The future patterns of scholarly communication lie in the hands of researchers in their capacity as creators, reviewers, editors and consumers of scholarly information. Scholars are unlikely to change publishing habits dramatically unless substantive arguments are promoted nationally or locally that will improve the exchange of knowledge with the accompanying accreditation support system.

Copyright ignorance or apathy is one of the main structural issues that impact upon repository deposit and thus scholarly communication change. Many authors that were identified in the UK RoMEO studies at www.lboro.ac.uk/departments/ls/disresearch/romeo/ revealed a lack of knowledge about their rights within publication frameworks, for example, whether their publications would be deposited in an institutional repository. There are a number of models that are now available, such as the Zwolle Principles at www.surf.nl/copyright/keyissues/scholarly-communication/principles.php and the ALPSP Model Agreement, which clearly provide exemplars for a better understanding of rights in a scholarly publishing environment.

Drahos and Braithwaite (2003) have argued for the major importance of intellectual property rights in the modern knowledge economy. They suggest that governments rarely take a cost-benefit approach to intellectual property and standards, which today are largely the product of the global strategies of a relatively small number of companies and business organizations that have realized the value of intellectual property sooner than anyone else.

As a counterpoint to this trend, Lawrence Lessig has argued for the creation of a Creative Commons (http://creativecommons.org/) as a common intellectual space. Lessig has defined four categories for licensing or authorizing the use of creative and intellectual work: attribution (author shares work, but requires right of attribution); non-commercial (author shares work but only for non-commercial use); derivative (author allows distribution but disallows derivative work); and Copyleft (share and share alike). This process allows a diversity of permissions in contrast to the present rigid framework of many commercial publishers. The future is likely to be evolutionary rather than revolutionary but changes in attitudes and scholarly communication models will ensure that intellectual feudalism will eventually be replaced by the global creative commons.

Lessig's Science Commons announced in 2004 (see http://creativecommons.org/projects/science/proposal) extends the boundaries into databases and patents, while the extension of the general programme into other countries, within their own copyright frameworks, is proving successful, for example the Australian Creative Commons at www.copyright.org.au/copysoc/NF04n02.pdf launched in March 2004. It is interesting to reflect here that the initiative for the Australian Creative Commons came partly from a former librarian who is now the Deputy Vice Chancellor of Queensland University of Technology (QUT). Librarians, or former librarians, have a significant role to play in the scholarly processes of publication as they have a wide vantage point, although many often do not have the necessary political infrastructure to ensure that change occurs.

One credo is to think globally and act locally. International collaborations provide resources outside an individual institution and can be applied either generically or within specific disciplines, the latter particularly important regarding the changing requirements of different disciplines. What is now required is a multidisciplinary approach, within overarching incentive frameworks, so that the research knowledge of the 21st century, currently trapped in 20th-century models, can be liberated for the citizens of the 21st century.

Another issue is the question of peer review. Peer review is an essential element in the context of Research Assessment Exercise processes. Peer review is often undertaken by the academic community as a result of what might be called 'misguided collegiality' – 'if I review an article in my subject area, someone else will do it for me in return'. However the system is coming under pressure as academics, increasingly under pressure themselves, have less time for qualitative refereeing and the reward system for peer review is often minimal or non-existent. Nonetheless, peer review is deemed by many as essential within the increasing number of open access journals.

Open access initiatives

A major phenomenon of the last two years is the open access movement. This focuses around the deposit of material in an open archive repository, for example of a subject or institution and the open access journal. It is not the purpose of this chapter to examine the various definitions of each initiative but rather to see them as symptoms of change within the scholarly publishing arena and to capitalize on the digital frameworks that currently exist or are going to be developed. The jury is still out on open access outcomes at the present time, but for Elsevier it is probably still only a small cloud in the blue skies of profits.

The debate in the magazine *Nature* in the first half of 2004 provides a variety of views from scientists, librarians, publishers and other stakeholders as to the various models, traditional and emerging, of scholarly publishing (Nature, 2004). One of the problems of the debates is that they often operate in closed circles, just as in the wider environment of the internet, gardeners talk to gardeners and science fiction fans talk to science fiction fans on e-mail lists or blogs. Many of the discussions reinforce opinions in closed gatherings or inflammatory confrontations.

This is particularly unhelpful in the long term when many of the assertions about scholarly publishing are not backed up by significant research data. Advocates of open access talk to each other, multinational publishers talk to their authors and report to their shareholders and academics rarely talk to anyone outside their discipline. This has been termed the 'sound of one hand clapping' (Steele, 2004). The ALPSP March 2004 seminar Scholarship-friendly Publishing provides a balanced view from the different constituent elements of the current scholarly publishing environment (Paulus, 2004). Open access, undoubtedly, can be seen as both an opportunity or a threat to scholarly and academic publishers (Lamb, 2004).

Governmental and societal statements

One of the key issues in this context will be to translate the governmental and societal statements of recent times into authorial change at the desktop. Libraries should play an active part in this process. The Berlin Declaration of October 2003 signed by all of Germany's principal scientific and scholarly institutions is only one example of such debate. It argues that the internet has fundamentally changed the practical and economic realities of distributing scholarly knowledge and cultural heritage with the guarantee of worldwide access. The Berlin signatories believe that in order to realize the vision of a global and accessible representation of knowledge a number of initiatives must be put in place. These include researchers and grant recipients being encouraged to publish their work according to the principles of open access; means and ways being developed to evaluate open access contributions in electronic journals and digital repositories within the standards of quality assurance including peer review. Suber (2004) has provided a cogent summary of the framework for 'creating an intellectual commons through open access'.

Further evidence of the dialogue at the highest policy level came from the high level OECD meeting of 34 countries held in Paris in late January 2004 (www.oecd.org/document/0,2340,en_2649_34487_25998799_1_1_1_1,00.html). The OECD Committee for Scientific and Technological Policy at Ministerial Level agreed that OECD countries will work towards 'the establishment of access regimes for digital research data from public funding' based on a set of objectives and principles including openness but also 'protection of intellectual property'. While this conference focused on scientific data it is no less pertinent to the universality of access to research results published in journals.

The difficulty of implementing change

There is clearly a framework at the highest governmental levels for action. The difficulties are going to be how these general sentiments, which might be simplified as 'public funding, public knowledge and public access', are going to be implemented when the vast majority of the academic community is still locked into historical scholarly reward systems that have more to do with history than the 21st century. The JISC Open Access survey published in 2004 noted that while almost two-thirds of respondents were aware of open access concepts, only 25% were made aware of this by their institutions. Academics indicated that if publishing work in an open access outlet was a condition of a research grant (and presumably also mandatory university policy) they would comply (Key Perspectives, 2004). If one changes the parameters and incentives, then practices may well change.

At present libraries pay to acquire scholarly knowledge on behalf of their institutions. With new open access models the role of the library could conceivably change. In terms of paying for open access journal contributions, the concept of the 'library as fiscal aggregator' has emerged. This involves an examination of the exchange of the library purchasing vote, or part thereof, into a model whereby the library pays to make available the intellectual output of the researchers of that institution. Cost models clearly need to be undertaken before major institutional shifts of resources can be contemplated.

The case for the 'public good' of institutional repositories and e-presses is a less difficult one to argue. Promoting the research output of the university through unified and federated repositories for the public good is no different from the input acquisition model?

The monograph and electronic scholarly publishing frameworks

With the development of institutional repositories and the branded output of universities in a digital environment, it is now perhaps appropriate to stand back and reconceptualize the creation and distribution of scholarly monographs. Here two trends are beginning to intersect, namely the 'decline' in university presses and the 'rise' of university libraries and information centres as electronic publishers.

The debate on serials in the sciences has overshadowed to date the crisis in monographic publishing. Global trends in academic book publishing, which indicate inter alia that a number of university publishers are facing a financial crisis, outlets for research monographs are drying up, print runs are being reduced and monograph costs are increasing (Steele, 2003). As serial costs take ever increasing shares of library budgets, research libraries spend less and less on monograph acquisitions.

The American Association of Research Libraries (ARL, 2001) has indicated that while world production of scholarly communication is estimated to have doubled since the mid 1980s, the average research library's monographic acquisitions have declined by 26%. This trend is particularly damaging for scholarship in the humanities and some of the social sciences and area studies. The announcement by ARL in 2004 of a partnership with the American Association of University Presses (http://aaupnet.org/arlaaup/) to collaborate on the visibility of presses on campus provides a foreshadowing of greater integration between libraries and presses in the future.

The dimension of e-presses and scholarly repositories is another development that has had and will have significant impact on university libraries and scholarly publishing. The future of the monograph in the electronic environment has engaged significant commentary in recent years, both from the perspective of the closure of traditional presses and the development of new e-presses and repositories. A pioneer in this process is California eScholarship whose material includes documents from preprints to electronic books (Tennant, 2003). This entails a model of graduated access to scholarship in which one can search in a federated manner across the repository to diverse material, such as peer-reviewed and non peer-reviewed, grey literature, digital theses, free electronic monographs and commercial books.

Another electronic publishing model but one, which deliberately attempts to incorporate the traditional scholarly accreditation process, is the Columbia University Gutenberg-e Project (www.gutenberg-e.org), a joint project with the American Historical Association. The Columbia initiative also includes within it the potential to transform the process of publication particularly in the context of collaborative teams and research output (Wittenberg, 2003). In this model, authors and editors share an electronic space in terms of creation. Wittenberg sees editors as becoming part of the front line, seeing their authors 'as active collaborators in creating new models rather than as lone toilers in specialized areas'.

In recent e-press developments libraries have played a significant role, for example, the Australian National University Press is located in the ANU library and electronic editors work closely with relevant library staff. In this way e-presses can build upon existing resources, such as the library and the IT divisions of a university, so that 'top-up' funding to establish repositories and e-presses for educational and research output is relatively small. This funding is not a simple exchange of funds from one bucket to another but the adoption of different philosophies.

An underlying motivation of the funding of the ANU E-Press was to provide a vehicle for the global distribution of ANU research, particularly for those areas in the humanities and social sciences who have suffered from the decline in university press production of scholarly monographs. This is particularly relevant in the case of young academics and research fellows who are trying get their first monograph published – still an essential step in gaining tenure. The Monash University E-Press has declared within its mission statement that its prime motivations include promotion of Monash University's research, teaching and intellectual capital and advanced scholarly communication by reducing costs and barriers to access.

It will be important to monitor the mutation of books in the electronic environment, particularly with the replication of electronic serial patterns. The Oxford Scholarship Online electronic monograph packages are available through consortia deals; chapters have individual abstracts and metadata provided by the author; and chapters can be downloaded into course packs. If this becomes a popular model, authors may subconsciously move from a continuous narrative stream and instead write in chapter 'bits'. We also need to be aware of the possible plight of the independent scholar if libraries end up with electronic versions only. Reading monographs through daily walk-in privileges will not be easy. Are we creating electronic ghettos on campuses with toll gates policed by institutional passwords? The deconstruction of the electronic monograph will provide new challenges, which are yet to be fully explored or debated.

Conclusion

The immediate future of scholarly publishing is likely to be a hybrid one with a number of models emerging and being tested in the evolving electronic distribution chains. It is unlikely that access to and distribution of top quality scientific information will change in the short term but the potential in the 'secondary ranks', and outside STM, could be significant. In that context, the creation, distribution and access to scholarly publishing is perhaps in a more fluid situation than has existed for many centuries.

We should not take for granted that the knowledge information frameworks will remain the same as in the past. Today's practices in scholarly publishing may only be the answers to yesterday's problems. Henry (2003) has noted that a panel debate on the future of academic publishing at the European Conference on Digital Libraries in Trondheim in 2003 was essentially a 20th-century one about electronic publishing rather than a 21st-century debate.

It may be also that we are unaware of new communication paradigms emerging, irrespective of the electronic habits of the upcoming 'Google generation'. For example, what is going to be the continuing impact of high speed electronic social networks and increasing numbers of 'blogs' and e-mails on scholarly communication patterns? Can accepted norms, such as peer review, be encompassed in such 'unwashed open access' communication forms? The immediacy of access and distribution will continue apace – it is just how the reward recognition process of scholarly publishing is incorporated into the new frameworks of scholarly communication.

These are some of the challenges being faced by libraries and universities in the first decade of the 21st century. Pre-Gutenberg libraries were scriptoriums in which the monks were responsible for the creation, copying and distribution of human knowledge, albeit in closed environments. It may well be that the digital environment sees a return to a library distribution role of scholarly knowledge and libraries will become the digitoriums of the 21st century.

References

Association of Learned and Professional Society Publishers (2002) *Authors and Electronic Publishing*, Worthing, ALPSP.

Association of Research Libraries (2001) Monograph and Serial Costs in ARL Libraries, 1986–2000, *ARL Bimonthly Report* 218, (October).

Chartered Institute of Library and Information Professionals (2004) Evidence submitted to the Science and Technology Committee Inquiry into Scientific Publications, http://opcit.eprints.org/feb19oa/royan-cilip-evidence.doc.

Cox, J. (2004) Submission to the UK House of Commons Inquiry on Scientific and Technical Publishing, www.biomedcentral.com/openaccess/inquiry/john_cox_associates.pdf.

Cox, J. and Cox, L. (2003) *Scholarly Publishing Practice: the ALPSP report on academic journal publishers' policies and practices in online publishing*, www.alpsp.org/publications/pub7.htm.

Crow, R. (2002) The Case for Institutional Repositories: a SPARC position paper, www.arl.org/sparc/IR/ir.html.

Drahos, P. and Braithwaite, J. (2003) *Information Feudalism: who owns the knowledge economy?*, London, Earthscan.

Harnad, S. (2003) Enhance UK Research Impact and Assessment by Making the RAE Webmetric, *Times Higher Education Supplement*, (6 June), www.ecs.soton.ac.uk/~harnad/Temp/thes.html.

Henry, G. (2003) Online Publishing in the 21st Century, *D-Lib Magazine*, (October), www.dlib.org/dlib/october03/henry/10henry.html.

Hey, T. (2004) Why Engage in E-science, *Update*, **3** (3), 25–7.

Hey, T. and Trefethen, A. (2003) The Data Deluge: an e-science perspective, www.rcuk.ac.uk/escience/documents/report_datadeluge.pdf.

Houghton, J., Steele, C. and Henty, M. (2003) *Changing Research Practices in the Digital Information and Communication Environment*, www.cfses.com/documents/Changing_Research_Practices.pdf.

Keller, M. (2004) Casting Forward Collection Development after Mass Digitization, Fiesole Collection Development Retreat, Florence, http://digital.casalini.it/retreat/2004_docs/KellerMichael.pdf.

Key Perspectives Limited (2004) JISC/OSI Journal Authors Survey Report,
www.jisc.ac.uk/uploaded_documents/JISCOAreport1.pdf.

Lamb, C. (2004) Open Access Publishing Models: opportunity or threat to
scholarly and academic publishers? *Learned Publishing*, **17** (2), 143–50.

Lougee, W. P. (2002) Diffuse Libraries: emergent roles for the research library
in the digital age, www.clir.org/pubs/abstract/pub108abst.html.

Lynch, C. (2003) Institutional Repositories: essential infrastructure for
scholarship in a digital age, *ARL Bimonthly Report*, (February),
www.arl.org/newsltr/226/ir.html.

Mabe, M. (2003) What Do Authors Care about? Fiesole Collection
Development Retreat, Oxford,
http://digital.casalini.it/retreat/2004_docs/Mabe.pdf.

Morgan, J. P. (2003) *Scientific and Medical Publishing*,
http://mm.jpmorgan.com.

Munroe, M. H. (2004) The Academic Publishing Industry: a story of merger
and acquisition, www.niulib.niu.edu/publishers/.

National Science Foundation (2004) *Knowledge Lost in Information: report of the
NSF Workshop on Research Directions for Digital Libraries, June 2003*,
www.sis.pitt.edu/~dlwkshop/JISC/NSFreport.pdf.

Nature (2004) Access to the Literature: the debate continues,
www.nature.com/nature/focus/accessdebate/.

Paulus, K. (2004) Scholarship-friendly Publishing, London, ALPSP Seminar,
www.alpsp.org/events/previous/s260304.htm.

Shiffrin, R. M. and Borner, K. (2004) Mapping Knowledge Domains,
Proceedings of the National Academy of Sciences, **101** (6 April), 5183–5.

Steele, C. (2003) Phoenix Rising: new models for the research monograph,
Learned Publishing, **16** (2), 111–22,
http://eprints.anu.edu.au/archive/00001032/.

Steele, C. (2004) The Sound of One Hand Clapping: the politics of scholarly
communication, The Second Nordic Conference on Scholarly
Communication, Lund, April, www.lub.lu.se/ncsc2004/.

Suber, P. (2004) *Creating an Intellectual Commons through Open Access*,
http://dlc.dlib.indiana.edu/archive/00001246/00/suber03304.pdf.

Tennant, R. (2003) *Rebirth of the Book*, Australian Academy of the Humanities,
National Maritime Museum, Sydney, March,
http://escholarship.cdlib.org/rtennant/presentations/2003oz/.

United Kingdom House of Commons Science and Technology Committee
    (2004) *Inquiry into Scientific Publications: evidence and submissions,*
    www.biomedcentral.com/openaccess/inquiry/.
Ware, M. (2004) Pathfinder Research on Web-based Repositories: final report,
    www.markwareconsulting.com.
Wittenberg, K. (2003) A New Model for Scholarly Publishing, *The Journal of
    Electronic Publishing,* **3** (4), www.press.umich.edu/jep/03-04/ciao.html.

4

Evolution or revolution in scholarly publishing: challenges to the publisher

John Cox

Introduction: a global industry in transition

Scholarly publishing has always been a global business. It has also always been a cottage industry. Although it is dominated by a small number of large commercial publishers (Elsevier, Springer Business + Media, Taylor & Francis, Wolters Kluwer, Wiley, Thomson, American Chemical Society and IEEE), over half of the industry is still in the hands of thousands of small publishers.

Writing in the UK, and knowing that the UK is home to a wide range of learned societies, which publish journals, and major commercial journal publishers such as Taylor & Francis, Oxford University Press, Cambridge University Press and Blackwell Publishing, as well as substantial UK publishing units of international companies such as Elsevier and Wiley, it is easy to forget that the UK is a very small part of the global market for scholarly literature.

The market is dominated by the USA. Morgan Stanley Equity Research Europe (2002) estimates that the USA accounts for 58% of scientific–technical–medical literature, Europe 26% and the rest of the world a mere 16%. What happens in the USA, as in so much else, affects the scholarly publishing business. As well as the growing doubt that has emerged during 2003 about the efficacy of the Big Deal as providing appropriate content and value for money, both publishers and librarians faced two other challenges, both originating in the USA but having a global impact. The first was the effect of the bankruptcy of a major player in the supply chain, RoweCom Inc. Corporate failures in business are by no means unusual, but are, mercifully, rare in scholarly publishing. The second was more fundamental: a serious challenge to the traditional subscription basis of journal publishing in the form of open access.

The gap between the growing scholarly literature and library budgets widens

It is important to remember that scholarly journals operate in a dysfunctional market. Price signals do not reach the customer. The reader may select but does not bear the cost of acquisition, while the library deploys the budget but is driven by readers' requirements. In parallel, library budgets have continued to deteriorate in relation to the volume of information they are expected to acquire.

In the 25 years following World War Two, investment in scientific research was substantial. During this period commercial journal publishers became significant players, as they were much more innovative in reacting to the resulting demand for scientific publishing capacity than the learned societies. At the same time, university education was rapidly expanding. The abundant resources for scientific research were matched by abundant funds for libraries collecting the resulting literature.

In the 1970s disillusionment set in. Science began to be seen as failing to deliver. It failed to solve the oil crisis in 1973. It has failed to show how we can avoid ecological disaster. We have turned away from nuclear weapons and nuclear energy. The popular regard for science in such areas as the genetic modification of crops or the safety of vaccines such as Measles Mumps Rubella is low. Nevertheless, the number of research and development staff has continued to grow in the last quarter century, albeit reverting to the growth rate of about 3% that prevailed before 1939. But while there are twice as many scientists in research as there were in 1975, publishing twice as many papers per year, library budgets have increased by only 40% during the period (Tenopir and King, 1997). The output of scientific papers is still growing at about 3% a year. Overall figures show that an increase of around 100 new peer-reviewed papers a year worldwide results in the launch of a new journal. New titles result from the growth of new fields – set against the decline of others – and the overall growth in the numbers of scientists and researchers.

In the 1970s library expenditure as a proportion of total university expenditure in the western world was running at 4% of total university expenditure. Since that time, that proportion has steadily declined. It is currently below 3%. It is simply undeniable that university libraries have not succeeded in selling the value of the library to the university community at large, and the faculty in particular. And faculty members have failed to support the one facility that provides them with the literature they need for scholarship and research. The problem in the UK is compounded by the consistent under-funding of higher education over many years, which by general agreement is some £8 billion less than it should be.

The Big Deal

One of the immediate effects of the advent of online journal publishing has been to release publishers and their customers from the straitjacket of individual journal subscription prices that apply to printed journals. In 1995 this manifested itself in Academic Press's IDEAL licence in which consortia of libraries were offered online access to the whole Academic Press list for an annual fee comprising the total expenditure on Academic Press journals by libraries in the consortium plus a premium of around 10%.

The benefits of the Big Deal in the early days were seen as positive. Usage dramatically increased. Usage was spread much more widely than the collection of titles to which the individual libraries previously subscribed. The early anecdotal evidence, from universities as geographically diverse as the University of Toronto in Canada, the University of Warwick in the UK and Macquarie University in Australia, was that where a complete list of journals is made available to readers, the pattern of usage did not follow the journals actually purchased by the library.

The US consortium OhioLINK found that, across its membership of 82 institutions from research libraries to public and school libraries, some 85% of usage came from 40% of the titles available online via OhioLINK, but that 52% of usage was from titles not previously held on subscription at the user's campus (Sanville, 2001).

After nearly a decade of the Big Deal, many librarians are more sceptical. They question the value of acquiring collections of journals that include many titles that are irrelevant to the disciplines in which teaching and research is actually undertaken in their institutions. They see the expense involved in cataloguing and establishing the linking mechanisms to such titles as wasteful. This scepticism has come into sharper focus as budgets have tightened. In surveys undertaken by the author in 2004 of academic librarians in the UK and the USA, the desire to return to individual title selection to reflect more accurately the needs of faculty and research was very striking.

The range and extent of Big Deals effected by major publishers has been criticized both by librarians and by smaller publishers as putting at risk smaller journal publishers by potentially excluding them from consortia purchases. Big Deals are difficult to get out of, and limit librarians' ability to select what is most appropriate for their readership. Publishers have reacted to this controversy by offering a multiplicity of different pricing models, based on simultaneous users, size and/or type of institution, and subject-based packages that are subsets of their journal lists. Some are also experimenting with 'self-select' packages in which discounts are offered on a sliding scale, depending on the number of titles ordered.

The Big Deal particularly threatens smaller publishers – especially learned societies – with only a handful of titles, albeit key titles in their respective disciplines. The marginalization of such smaller publishers is a concern shared not only by the publishers themselves but also by academic libraries worried about the sustainability of important titles that represent value for money. There are a number of initiatives that are attempting to compete with such deals by forming coalitions of small publishers, for example the Association of Learned and Professional Society Publishers' Learned Journal Collection (UK) and BioOne (USA). In the case of the former, the ALPSP, the UK-based trade association representing scholarly publishers, took the initiative to create a frame-work within which smaller ALPSP member publishers work together, through Swets Information Services, to sell a combined package of their journals to consortia and other large customers. ALPSP and Swets have already announced the completion of five significant licences.

The collapse of RoweCom

In 2003 the effects of the collapse of RoweCom, one of the principal international subscription agents, with a strong market position in the USA became clear.

Ten years ago libraries had a great deal of choice of subscription agents with which they could place their journal acquisitions, but in the last decade there has been a process of concentration in this part of the scholarly publishing supply chain. Blackwell's and Faxon Europe's busi-nesses were both swallowed by Swets. EBSCO and Swets bought up many of their smaller brethren, and Faxon, in financial difficulties in 1994, was successively acquired by Dawson and then RoweCom. RoweCom itself was acquired by divine Inc. In 2002 both RoweCom and divine Inc. entered bankruptcy, as a result of which the remnants of the RoweCom business became part of EBSCO.

The Faxon/RoweCom business had been in financial difficulties or had changed hands in uncertain circumstances three times before bank-ruptcy struck. In spite of the evidence, and industry speculation at con-ferences and exhibitions, both publishers and librarians continued to trade with Faxon/RoweCom throughout the 1990s.

The scholarly publishing business operates to a large extent on trust. Most major subscription agents have always operated 'pre-payment plans', which enabled libraries to prepay the following year's journal subscriptions on an agreed estimate, as early as April or May of the prior year. The library benefited by earning interest on the money that was prepaid, or by receiving a discount on subscriptions at renewal time that would depend on how far in advance the pre-payment was made. This system has always operated in the confidence that the subscription agents themselves were impeccably honest and financially sound. The pre-payment monies were never put in trust or in escrow accounts; they simply became part of their normal cash flow.

There was never any objective reason why vendors should be immune to the vicissitudes of business and financial life. Nevertheless, the system worked, until the established journal supply chain started to face stresses and strains brought out by two significant changes in trading conditions that emerged in the 1990s: eroding operating margins and the emergence of online journal publishing.

Operating margins eroded

Being a subscription agent has always depended on wafer-thin margins. In the early 1990s most vendors' gross margin – the difference between what was received from libraries and what was paid to publishers – was between 8 and 9%: roughly 2–3% from libraries in the form of a service charge, and 6% from publisher discounts. Some publishers gave a 10% discount, while others – notably US learned societies – gave no discount at all. Since that time, the larger publishers have reduced their discounts from a comfortable 10% to a much less comfortable 5%. Moreover, subscription agents found it impossible to increase their service charges to libraries to compensate for this loss of operating margin because of the competition between them for new business. An almost suicidal price war between the agents took hold in the mid 1990s. By 2000 library service charges had virtually disappeared.

Subscription agents have been their own worst enemies in this. They have continued to provide technology services to libraries at no cost, and they have competed with each other on price, eroding their gross margins to levels below survival. Buying business is the shortcut to bankruptcy. And the first to face real financial difficulty were always going to be those with management instability and the least sound finances.

The emergence of online journal publishing

Online journal publishing began in 1995, changing the role of subscription agents. They found it very difficult to make the change from being library-focused procurement agents to being transaction and service partners in the online environment. They were saddled with a legacy of business practices from the print environment. But what was going to count was how vendors adapt to new circumstances.

In the mid 1990s subscription agents did not know how to reposition their business as publishers sought their assistance in marketing bright new technology. From the publishers' viewpoint, they were established trading partners; working together in the online environment would merely extend that relationship. The problem was that publishers expected them to sell their particular products, while they have always maintained neutrality between different publishers, with their sales efforts being directed at selling their procurement and transaction services, rather than journals themselves. Only now – seven or eight years later – have the major subscription agents put themselves in a position to be a positive help to publishers.

Their position was made more difficult by some of the larger publishers wishing to deal directly with libraries over online journals. Publishers wanted to understand this new market, which meant that they had to engage directly with libraries, rather than mediating contact through a third party. Indeed, many library consortia want to deal directly as well. The view in the early days was that the organ grinder was a better contact than the monkey. Negotiations are better handled face to face than through third parties. The provision of online journals raises performance, compatibility, technical support and customer service issues that simply do not apply in the print world. These issues arise in implementing an online journal licence and are best dealt with directly, rather than via a third party. The die was cast in those early days.

The problem for subscription agents was that those early direct deals usually involved large publishers, whose journals were relatively expensive, relatively easy to process and who gave a reasonable level of discount. The loss of such traffic leaves the agent with a journal mix of less expensive – so the discount would be less valuable – journals that were more difficult and time consuming – expensive – to process and service. The economic facts of life looked even more difficult.

Lessons to be learned from the collapse of RoweCom

What was remarkable in these circumstances was that neither publishers nor librarians – especially US academic librarians, who comprised the core of RoweCom's customer base – appeared to take any step to forestall a looming crisis. Even more remarkable, many librarians continued to place their faith in RoweCom, and make substantial pre-payments even when other subscription agents and many publishers were questioning RoweCom's financial health. Those librarians wanted to believe that RoweCom continued to operate as Faxon used to – the academic vendor of choice for most US universities.

Normal business prudence dictates that any organization should conduct regular financial health checks on their suppliers or trading partners. It is standard practice in the public and private sectors to check the financial provenance of a supplier. This can be done by asking for the supplier's accounts (usually for the previous three years), or obtaining accounts filed with the stock exchange in the case of public companies, or obtaining accounts filed with the public authorities, where this applies. Credit reports can be obtained from reputable specialist companies such as Dun & Bradstreet or ICC. The finance department of any organization should be able to do this. Not to undertake elementary financial checks before paying large sums of money to subscription agents under a pre-payment plan is the height of irresponsibility. In most commercial environments, it would be treated as such, and lead to disciplinary action, including dismissal.

The result of the RoweCom bankruptcy has been that EBSCO has acquired the RoweCom business, at the cost of bearing a significant administrative and financial burden to ensure that libraries continued to receive their journals, and publishers received at least some of the subscription revenue due to them. Publishers have taken a significant loss on the business transacted through RoweCom in the USA, while continuing to supply libraries with 2003 issues. The libraries have been insulated from the consequences of the failure.

One thing that has educated and appalled all observers of the sad demise of what had been one of the leading vendors worldwide is the time and the administrative burden involved in establishing creditors' claims against RoweCom and divine. In typical liquidations, the creditors are lucky to see 10 cents on the dollar. In this case, the recovery may be significantly better than that. But that is scant comfort to publishers, whether commercial or non-profit, who have seen their financial performance badly compromised.

So what is the principal lesson to be drawn from this experience? It is the most basic of business lessons: check out those companies that supply products and services. Neither libraries nor publishers are likely to escape so lightly if there is a next time. Credit or financial health checks are vital: they should become a normal feature of the process of trade. To do otherwise is to assume a risk that is unnecessary and financially irresponsible.

The formidable challenge of open access

The past year has been marked by a fundamental challenge to the way journal publishing has traditionally operated. The open access movement has gathered a head of steam, and has certainly engaged the attention of librarians and many researchers. Scholarly journal publishing is driven by the needs of authors to publish. Indeed, journals are seen as the 'minutes of science'; research has not been completed until it has been published. The pressure to publish is increased by the quality audit processes, like the UK's Research Assessment Exercise, that are now applied by government agencies in may countries. As a supply-driven activity, there is much to be said for the business model on which it is based, to be funded where the demand actually lies: on the author, rather than on the reader.

Open access is a term used to describe a number of publishing models, all of which intend to remove the traditional journal subscription model. Recognized definitions of open access have been developed by a number of organizations, including the two below.

The Bethesda Statement (2003)

An Open Access Publication[1] is one that meets the following two conditions:

The author(s) and copyright holder(s) grant(s) to all users a free, irrevocable, world-wide, perpetual right of access to, and a license to copy, use, distribute, transmit and display the work publicly and to make and distribute derivative works, in any digital medium for any responsible purpose, subject to proper attribution of authorship,[2] as well as the right to make small numbers of printed copies for their personal use.

A complete version of the work and all supplemental materials, including a copy of the permission as stated above, in a suitable standard electronic format is deposited immediately upon initial publication in at least one online repository that is supported by an academic institution, scholarly society, government agency, or other well-established organization that seeks to enable open access, unrestricted distribution, interoperability, and long-term archiving.

Notes:

1   Open access is a property of individual works, not necessarily journals or publishers.
2   Community standards, rather than copyright law, will continue to provide the mechanism for enforcement of proper attribution and responsible use of the published work, as they do now.

(Bethesda Statement, 2003)

The Budapest Open Access Initiative (2001)

By 'open access' to this literature we mean its free availability on the public internet, permitting any users to read, download, copy, distribute, print, search, or link to the full texts of these articles, crawl them for indexing, pass them as data to software, or use them for any other lawful purpose, without financial, legal or technical barriers other than those inseparable from gaining access to the internet itself. The only constraint on reproduction and distribution, and the only role for copyright in this domain, should be to give authors control over the integrity of their work and the right to be properly acknowledged and cited.   (Budapest Open Access Initiative 2001)

Regardless of differences in detail between different statements and manifestos on open access, the common feature is the desire for unfettered availability online to peer-reviewed research papers upon publication. This may involve a combination of all or any of the following:

• Authors retain copyright and permits their work to be freely available online (this is in contrast to the conventional publishing process in which authors assign copyright, or grant exclusive publishing rights in all media, to the publisher, which then manages access to the published work).
• The article is published in an open access journal.
• The article is posted to an institutional or discipline-based online depository for free online access, even though it may be published in a conventional subscription-based journal.

In the discussions and position papers adopted by many open access advocates, there appears to be a choice of two routes to open access: the development of open access journals, and the posting of published papers in institutional or discipline-based depositories, which are freely accessible in parallel with formal publication in a journal.

Open access journals

Open access journals form a very small part of current scientific journal literature: some 800 titles out of 18,669 active English language peer-reviewed academic and scholarly titles (Ulrich's, 2004). Access to open access journals is entirely free online and worldwide. They do not rely on the traditional subscription-based model to generate revenue; revenue is generated in one, or both, of two ways:

1 The author's institution or research grant pays a publication fee, upon acceptance of the article, which covers the article selection process, peer review, the production process and online publication.
2 Institutions pay an annual membership fee to the open access journal, which allows an unlimited number of articles accepted for publication from authors at that institution to be published in the journal. The institutional membership is now offered by Public Library of Science and BioMed Central, two of the principal open access journal publishers.

The difficulty faced by open access journals is to persuade an author to submit a paper to an unproven open access title and pay for the privilege, instead of an established high-impact journal that will publish the paper at no charge to the author. That is a challenging sales pitch to make. Authors seeking tenure, promotion or grant allocation are judged on their publishing record, in which the status of the journal in which they are published is an important factor; they have to publish in reputable, high impact journals. Furthermore, there are three issues that must be addressed in judging whether a transition to open access journals will serve the scholarly community well:

1 At present, non-academic purchases comprise some 25% of journal revenues – corporate, government and other non-academic libraries – while non-academic authors are much less significant as a proportion of total authorship. If open access journals establish themselves, these libraries will access the literature free of charge. The academic community will have to bear almost the entire burden of financing the publishing cycle. Even if open access publishing is less expensive than the subscription-based model, the advantage to the academy is lost by excluding revenue from corporate and other sources.
2 Many learned societies depend on publishing revenues to finance other member activities – seminars, conferences, and so on. Open access may well destroy the financial underpinning of most learned society activities.
3 Much of the information infrastructure that publishers and librarians have developed over many years will remain necessary so that the literature emanating from a fragmented publishing industry can be indexed, navigated, searched, accessed and linked together in an effective information service. Some open access advocates talk of 'scholarly skywriting' (Harnad, n.d.) and confuse the formal publishing process with the full range of communication between scientists, which has always been a feature of the research community. It is not explained how this unstructured, anarchical approach to disseminating the 'minutes of science' benefits science.

There is a very slight risk that open access publishing, in which authors or their agents fund publication, may weaken the integrity of peer review. If the publishing process is funded by the author, there is a potential for the exercise of undue influence on editors anxious to build the flow of papers for publication in their journals. In the current subscription-based publishing system, the flow of money is wholly divorced from the process of review and acceptance for publication. In open access publishing, the flow of money to support the enterprise is very closely linked to acceptance for publication.

The open archive

Open archives, self-archiving and institutional repositories are important components of the open access movement. Open archiving has often been described as being the same thing as institutional repositories and the self-archiving of pre-print articles. In reality, the picture is considerably more complex. There are a number of guises in which open archives appear:

- Authors simply post their articles as accepted for publication to their personal web pages.
- Articles are posted to an institutional depository: a server established by a university or research organization to host the output of the institution's faculty and researchers.
- Articles are posted to an open depository established to cover a specific discipline.

Posting published papers to an institutional depository in parallel with formal publication involves financing a parallel information system. It requires the establishment of appropriate servers in each university and the probable enhancement of connectivity to the internet. Most important of all, it requires the active participation of authors. In the ALPSP survey it was found that, while most publishers require authors to transfer copyright, most also allow published articles to be posted to websites; they are more inclined to allow posting published articles to the author's own site than their institution's (although retrieval technology makes the difference between the two minimal). Few publishers disallow the re-use of authors' material within the academic institution, subject to proper acknowledgement of the journal and publisher. Publishers are not inhibiting posting to institutional depositories; authors have, in general, not yet been persuaded that this is a desirable thing to do.

Uncertainties about the open access model

It is not inappropriate at this stage to be in the position of a sceptic, if only because open access is unproven as a sustainable business model and also because the enthusiasts for open access tend to describe its advantages in quasi-religious language rather than in objective systemic and organizational terms. There are practical problems in making the transition from the current subscription-based business model to an open access model where the financial burden falls on authors or their agents in the form of the university or research funding agency.

The first and foremost uncertainty created in open access publishing is the place of copyright. The Budapest Open Access Initiative states that open access publishing is entirely compatible with copyright law, in that it gives the copyright holder the right to make access open or restricted; however, it seeks to put copyright in the hands of the author or institution that wishes to make access open. This initiative negates the traditional role of the publisher as midwife to and curator of scholarly literature and removes the basis upon which they have operated their businesses until now.

The implication of authors' retention of copyright is that the only 'properties' the publisher is left holding are the journal 'brand' and all of the added value that they can attach to the content. Authors are able to do what they want with their article: post it to open archives, institutional and discipline specific repositories. The journal brand is still of great importance to editors and to authors in terms of tenure and promotion. Added value services such as metadata, portals, usage statistics, search functions and packages can continue to be provided by the publisher as an alternative to the subscription to the content of any journals or databases. Apart from any revenue generated from publication fees, added value services will be the remaining core of the publisher's business.

It is generally accepted that peer review is provided by academics without any remuneration; it is seen as part of the responsibilities of research and scholarship. In fact, many publishers do provide payment to their reviewers, although it is often nominal. But peer review involves considerable administration, which is traditionally performed or facilitated and funded by the publisher. In other words, the system of peer review has to be funded. This has been recognized by open access advocates.

Open access involves shifting the cost of publication, including peer review, from the individual or institutional subscriber to the author, by charging the author a publication fee. As proposed by open access advocates, this fee covers the cost of operating the publication, including the cost of processing and reviewing papers that are rejected. The rejection rate in leading, highly respected journals can be as high as 70–80% of all papers submitted. If the author whose paper is accepted for publication bears the whole cost of publication, this means that author bears the cost of processing papers that are rejected; it seems inequitable that a successful author should bear the costs involved in dealing with others whose work is judged not to be worthy of publication. This will result in the most prestigious journals being the most expensive. Alternatively, open access journals must begin to charge a submission fee, where the author has no guarantee that their paper is going to be published. This may be met with some objection from the academic community.

Open access journals that charge institutions a membership fee may also encounter financial difficulties. The membership fee does not take into account the number of submissions (and therefore rejections) made by any one institution. This causes the cost of peer review of articles from that one institution potentially to spiral upwards, making the membership fee inadequate to cover these costs.

The advocates of open access have failed to address a range of costs involved in open access systems to facilitate access and linking. It is unclear how the infrastructure will be funded:

1 Technology is frequently advancing and changing. Major upgrades to systems that will provide open access will cost large sums of money. It is assumed that open access will create more use, and many believe that users will find articles using robots or harvesting tools that

require considerable bandwidth and processing capacity.

2 In order to integrate open access journal articles into the existing body of research literature online, they will have to be allocated digital object identifiers (DOIs), linked to CrossRef and be Open URL compliant; metadata will have to be created, and usage statistics generated.

3 Potential readers need to know of the existence of open access journals and repositories. This requires systematic marketing. Successfully reaching an entire academic community takes time and incurs a number of costs, whether this marketing is online, at conferences or paper-based (direct mail).

Making the transition

Authors need to publish in order to establish their 'ownership' of their research and to derive their rewards in the form of career progression and funding for further research. If one were to design a publishing system on a blank sheet of paper, there is some merit in meeting the costs of that system at the point of supply, rather than, as at present, at the point of delivery. However, open access has to displace a publishing system based on subscriptions that has survived for 300 years. The key area in which open access may fail is during the transitional period from the present system. This is dependent on persuading academic authors to submit their papers to largely unproven open access journals – and pay for the privilege – rather than to established journals.

In order for open access journals to reach a significant standard of prestige and attract papers from authors up for tenure or promotion, they need to be recognized by the whole academic community they serve. This inevitably involves the cost of marketing and technology maintenance, which is not necessarily covered by the modest publication fee. Furthermore, even after initial marketing, it will still take time for a journal to be recognized as prestigious. Whether open access journals can be sustained for this transitional period remains to be seen.

If open archives are to succeed on any level, those authors publishing in traditional journals must then be given permission by the publisher to post the peer-reviewed version of the article in open archives or repositories. There has been a great deal of activity in establishing repositories, not only in the USA but also in Australia and the UK. These initiatives have been primed by foundation or government money. This does not necessarily guarantee the sustainability of the publication model.

Will open access displace the current publishing system?

Open access, though unproven, represents a significant challenge to the existing publishing paradigm. The level of concern that the current market for journals is not working properly is shared not only by many librarians and academics, but also by governments and funding agencies. Some key points and questions to consider about the future of open access are summarized below:

1 Will open access journals survive the transitional period, when many authors will be disinclined to publish in them due to the demands of tenure and promotion? Will they be sustainable without making the publication fee, or indeed a submission fee, unpalatable to the authors and institutions, while those same institutions are still maintaining traditional journal subscriptions?
2 Traditional publishers may decide to stop charging for articles and other content. They may charge publication fees to cover peer review and may then sell their packages – or indeed individual online journals – as the added value services that are integral to these products. Access to actual articles remains open, but libraries will require the functionality that their patrons have come to expect.
3 Many publishers already allow to authors to post peer-reviewed versions of their articles to their institution's repository as 'post-prints', or to discipline-based depositories. While there is no current evidence that this practice has affected subscriptions, if the use of such repositories becomes widespread, will journal subscriptions start to fall and will publishers in turn need to re-invent themselves?

The fundamental issue of the sustainability of an open access publishing model remains unanswered. Around 800 open access journals are listed in the Lund University directory at www.doaj.org. With the exception of around 100 titles from BioMed Central, the majority of them have been started by enthusiasts within university departments. Such journals depend on the commitment of the early adopters of the open access model. Their sustainability depends on generating ongoing revenue to meet all the costs associated with publishing a journal, including staff, technology, marketing, peer review and publication. While many are beneficiaries of grant money, open access publishing must develop a wholly sustainable business model in order to continue operating.

Conclusion: what will authors want?

The advocates of open access have been very active in stressing how the demand for open access is growing from both authors and readers. Undoubtedly its supporters are very vocal. Nevertheless, there is some doubt about how far demand has actually grown – crucially, beyond the early adopters of open access into the wider scholarly author community. A recent small survey (www.jisc.ac.uk/uploaded_documents/ JISCOAreport1.pdf) carried out for JISC/OSI of two matching groups of authors ('traditional' journal authors and open access authors) found that open access is no more attractive to young authors or to established authors. The level of awareness of open access journals was low, and of institutional depositories even lower. A much larger research project undertaken by the Centre for Information Behaviour and the Evaluation of Research (CIBER) at City University, London, reinforced the view that the level of awareness of open access in the author community is low (ALPSP, 2004).

On the other hand, Oxford University Press (2004) has reported that its open access experiment with a special January 2004 issue of *Nucleic Acids Research* has been deemed so successful that it will be repeated for the July 2004 issue. In January 2004 142 papers were published, with an author fee of £300. Only 10% requested that the fee be waived.

So far as the other strand of open access is concerned, there is still little evidence that open archives are being widely used by authors, especially institutional repositories. The Publishers and Libraries Solutions (PALS) Group in the UK commissioned a survey in 2003 of institutional repositories. Some 45 repositories were examined. Most were found to be at an embryonic stage, with little content in them, and no evidence that they will develop into substantial interoperable depositories of published journal literature (Ware, 2004).

So the author community is clearly ill-informed about the practicalities of open access. The rhetoric is alive and kicking. It is clearly making headway in the life sciences. As yet, it appears to have had little effect on author behaviour in most other disciplines. Nevertheless, there is a cautionary analogy to be drawn from the airline industry. Most airlines (now known rather charmingly as the 'legacy carriers') assumed that low cost airlines like South West or Ryanair would never affect their own operations. But the low cost carriers re-engineered the process of operating air transport services, and seized on the internet as the principal distribution mechanism for selling tickets. We now know that new entrants into an industry can revolutionize the ways things are done. It would be a foolish publisher who discounted open access as an alternative model for the future and assumed that their business is immune to change.

References

Association of Learned and Professional Society Publishers (2004) ALPSP Alert (81), www.aplsp.org.

Bethesda Statement on Open Access Publishing (2003), www.earlham.edu/~peters/fos/bethesda.htm.

Budapest Open Access Initiative (2001) www.earlham.edu/~peters/fos/boaifaq.htm.

Harnad, S. (n.d.) Prima-Facie FaQs for Overcoming Zeno's Paralysis, www.ecs.soton.ac.uk/~harnad/Tp/resolution.htm#8.

Morgan Stanley Equity Research Europe (2002) Scientific Publishing: knowledge is power, London, 1–20, www.econ.ucsb.edu/~tedb/Journals/morganstanley.pdf.

Oxford University Press (2004) Press release, 18 February, www3.oup.co.uk/jnls/2004/02/18/index.html.

Sanville, T. (2001) A Method out of the Madness: OhioLINK's collaborative response to the serials crisis – a progress report, *Serials Librarian*, **40** (1/2), 129–55.

Tenopir, C. and King, D. W. (1997) Trends in Scientific Scholarly Journal
    Publishing in the United States, *Journal of Scholarly Publishing*, **28** (3),
    135–70.
Ulrich's Periodicals Directory (2004) www.ulrichsweb.com.
Ware, M. (2004) Pathfinder Research on Web-based Repositories,
    www.palsgroup.org.uk.

ACCESS AND PRESERVATION INITIATIVES IN SCHOLARLY PUBLISHING

5

Access and usability issues of scholarly electronic publications

Gobinda G. Chowdhury

Introduction

Scholarly communications can take place through a number of documentary forms including seminar and conference papers, technical reports, theses and dissertations, journal articles and review papers, monographs, edited books, and so on. Users in today's digital library world can gain access to these scholarly publications through a variety of channels, ranging from the websites of the producers or publishers of the information resources to a number of intermediaries and service providers, search tools and services. But with so many alternatives available to them, users often find it difficult to choose the best option to access the scholarly information they need. Each channel has its own policies and techniques for the identification, organization and retrieval of information resources, and these not only influence the usability of the services, but also the output that the users are likely to get at the end of a search session.

Usability and user friendliness of information access systems depend on a number of factors. Traditionally access to scholarly electronic publications was provided by specialized agencies that included database producers or publishers and online search service providers such as Dialog. In the past a number of researchers have studied the usability and user friendliness of electronic information services. However, these issues have recently become more critical for a number of reasons, mainly because access to scholarly information is no longer controlled by the specialized agencies. In fact, in theory anyone can be an information producer and information service provider in the current environment of web and digital libraries. While this phenomenon increases the opportunities for the users, it also creates a number of problems and confusion.

This chapter looks at the various access and usability issues related to scholarly information resources. It first looks at the various channels through which a user can get access to scholarly electronic publications. It then discusses the issues and studies surrounding usability. Some important parameters for measuring the usability of information access systems have been identified. Finally the chapter looks at the major problems facing users in gaining access to scholarly information through today's hybrid libraries, and mentions some possible measures to resolve them.

Channels for access to scholarly information

Users can now access scholarly information resources through a number of documentary forms and channels, such as:

- full texts of journals – printed as well as electronic – through the publisher, such as Emerald, or through service providers, such as Ingenta
- e-journals and e-books – usually through the publisher's website or through services such as subject gateways (see below)
- digital libraries – general or institutional – websites of specific digital libraries such as the California Digital Library, American Computing Machinery (ACM) digital library, New Zealand Digital Library (NZDL) and National Science Digital Library (NSDL)
- digital libraries of special collections such as Networked Digital Library of Theses and Dissertations (NDLTD) and Alexandria digital library (a digital library of spatial information resources)

- CD-ROM and traditional online databases – through publishers and/or service providers such as Dialog and Ovid
- subject gateways – Social Science Information Gateway (SOSIG), OMNI (health information gateway), Biz/ed (business information gateway), EEVL (subject gateway for engineering, mathematics and computing), and so on
- web search tools – directories (such as Yahoo!), search engines including meta and specialized search engines (such as Google, AskJeeves, Kartoo and Vivisimo)
- special initiatives such as JSTOR and EDINA
- publicly available scholarly information archives such as arxiv.org (commonly known as the Los Alamos E-Print Archives), Cognitive Sciences Eprint Archive (CogPrints) and Networked Computer Science Technical Reference Library (NCSTRL)
- hybrid libraries – library web pages such as the one for the Strathclyde University library (www.lib.strath.ac.uk)
- specific websites of institutions, professional bodies and funding agencies on specific subjects, for example IFLANET, Text Retrieval Conferences (TREC) and Digital Library Initiatives (DLI)
- personal websites – those of specific persons providing access to some or all of their own publications, and so on.

While some of these services are available for free, others offer controlled access – through registration and payment. Nevertheless, the internet and digital libraries have brought a significant change to the mechanisms of information access and use. In most cases users no longer need to pay for browsing or searching an information collection, while in others even access to full text scholarly publications is available without charge. This has of course brought many challenges, the most prominent of which are related to usability issues.

The impact of the web on information access systems

Internet computing has made a tremendous impact on the technological and economic aspects of information access. For example, the internet has made it possible to access virtually any type of information located anywhere in the world. A number of web search tools have been built over the past few years that are not only robust but also sophisticated. In fact, some of the improvements in information access that have taken place since the mid 1990s surpass the developments in this field over the previous three decades. Improvements in web information retrieval are taking place very fast, and the most interesting point is that end-users do not have to pay for these developments. Before the internet era, information retrieval experiments and evaluation used to take place on small test collections that were tiny in comparison with the size of the web. Indeed, this was one of the major criticisms of information retrieval experiments of that time.

Web search tools have also brought major changes in the economics that prevailed in the information industry for several decades. Before the internet, users had to pay to use search engines as well as for content. Web search tools are free at the point of use, and yet they are constantly improving their performance through research and innovation. Many information search services now offer free browse and search options for their collections.

The web has facilitated the creation and redesign of many information access channels including online journals and service providers, e-books, digital libraries and online databases and search services. Sophisticated web search interfaces to e-journals, databases and digital libraries are now commonplace, but this was unthinkable even a decade ago. However, despite having all these sophisticated information access systems, the fundamental question still remains: is it easy to get access to the right information at the right time with minimum resources and effort? Borgman (2000) comments that, despite the technological advances, information systems continue to be difficult to use. This chapter revisits this issue in the context of obtaining access to electronic scholarly information resources.

Usability

'Usability' and 'user friendliness' are two closely related concepts and are often used interchangeably in the information science literature. Many researchers, especially those who are from the human-computer interaction (HCI) community, define usability in relation to the user interface. For example, Hansen (1998) comments that the concept of usability is related to the effectiveness and efficiency of the user interface, and also to the user's reactions to that interface. Nielsen (1993) suggests that user friendliness consists of several factors such as simplicity of learning, efficiency of use, simplicity of memorizing, and so on.

Usable systems are those that enable users to perform a set of specified tasks within a specified environment effectively and easily. The 'usability' of an information service (more precisely a channel providing access to one or more types of information resources) is generally taken to mean how easily the service can be used to get access to the required information. As soon as we accept this simple definition, we come across some major issues concerning information services. First, it should be easy to use the service. A number of technical issues are involved here, including interface design, retrieval mechanisms, interoperability where multiple channels and/or databases are involved, and so on. Another issue, often ignored, is related to the user: it is highly impractical to design a service that can be used with equal ease by all kinds of users around the world, and yet this is what most of today's digital information services aim to accomplish. This in turn leads to other issues in connection with the objectives and functionality of each information service.

Another factor relates to the information that users are looking for. In our definition above we have assumed that an information service should be such that it can be used easily to get access to required information. This term 'required information' brings up a number of critical issues that in turn influence usability. Most information services operate on the assumption that users are able to specify correctly the information that they require. In fact this is often a major difficulty, since research in human information behaviour shows that often users find it difficult to specify clearly what they need, and moreover their information needs often change in the course of an information search session (Borgman, 2000; Chowdhury, 2004). In other words, we assess the usability of information services using a parameter that is itself difficult to define. Moreover, in today's digital environment, the user can be anyone, virtually anywhere in the world, and this poses more problems for the designers of information services, because ideally one should try to design a service that can satisfy every possible user's information requirements, despite their linguistic, cultural and various other socio-economic differences.

Usability studies and guidelines

Perspectives on usability have shifted substantially over the past few decades – initially the purpose of ergonomics was to shape human beings to adapt to the technology, whereas now designers try to alter the technology to suit human capabilities and needs (Borgman, 2000). Many recent studies have examined the usability of electronic information services. Some of these studies were designed to assess the performance of a specific system, while others aimed to develop evaluation metrics and guidelines.

Many guidelines for the usability of websites and website design have appeared in the last few years (see for example, Palmer, 2002; White, 2002; Byerley and Chambers, 2002; Brinck, Gergle and Wood, 2001; Hert, Jacob and Dawson, 2000. Those studying the usability of information services for users with special needs comment that commercial databases should conduct usability testing with users who rely on screen readers for access to the web. A number of studies have examined user interfaces, a field that is closely related to the usability of electronic information services. Several studies since 2000 have focused on the usability of digital libraries. Some such studies are discussed in the following sections.

Usability and user interfaces

User interfaces to information retrieval systems that support information-seeking processes have been widely discussed in the literature. Interface design encompasses what appears on the user's screen, how they view it and how they manipulate it. Interface design thus has a tremendous impact on usability. Marchionini (1992) provides a description of the essential features of interfaces to support end-user information seeking and suggests five information-seeking functions: problem definition, source selection, problem articulation, result examination and information extraction. He argues that much of the interface work has focused on articulating problems (including formulating queries) and that the other functions need to be investigated in designing information-seeking interfaces. Marchionini and Komlodi (1998) discuss the evolution of interfaces and trace research and development in three areas: information seeking, interface design and computer technology. Savage-Knepshield and Belkin (1999) discuss the interface design challenges within the context of information retrieval interaction over the last three decades. They note that the degree of interaction between the searcher and the IR system has dramatically increased and much research is still required to meet the challenges in interface design for IR interaction. Hearst (1999) discusses user interface support for the information-seeking process and describes the features of these interfaces that aid such processes as query formulation and specification, viewing results and interactive relevance feedback. She points out that there is increasing interest in taking the behaviour of individuals into account when designing interfaces.

Hilbert and Redmiles (2000) report on a survey that examines computer-aided techniques used by HCI practitioners and researchers to extract usability-related information from user interfaces. Researchers in the HCI Lab in the University of Maryland (n.d.) have developed the following generic guidelines for the design of user interfaces to information systems:

- consistency with respect to the use of word(s), objects, and standards
- proper positioning of objects for task performance, comprehensibility, information density and aesthetics
- an appropriate mix of graphical user interface (GUI) objects
- user interaction logging for analysis of usage patterns.

Shneiderman and his associates propose the following guiding principles for design of user interfaces that will help improve the usability of the underlying information access systems (Shneiderman, Byrd and Croft, 1997, 1998; Shneiderman, 1998):

- Strive for consistency in terminology, layout, instructions, fonts and colour.

- Provide shortcuts for skilled users.
- Provide appropriate and informative feedback about the sources and what is being searched for.
- Design for closure so that users know when they have completed searching the entire collection or have viewed every item in a browse list.
- Permit reversal of actions so that users can undo or modify actions; for example, they should be able to modify their queries or go back to the previous stage in a search session.
- Support user control, allowing users to monitor the progress of a search and be able to specify the parameters to control a search.
- Reduce short-term memory load: the system should keep track of some important actions performed by the users and allow them to jump easily to a formerly performed action, for example, to a former query or to a specific result set.
- Provide simple error-handling facilities to allow users to rectify errors easily; all error messages should be clear and specific.
- Provide plenty of space for entering text in search boxes.
- Provide alternative interfaces for expert and novice users.

Usability of digital libraries

Digital libaries can be evaluated on three key components: content, functionality and user interface (Van House et al, 1996). A number of recent studies have examined the usability of digital libraries and the HCI community always emphasizes the usability of user interfaces. Their usability testing involves assessing the effectiveness, efficiency and/or satisfaction of the user with a particular interface (Choudhury, Hobbs and Lorie, 2002; Norlin, 2000; Nielsen, 1993). Bollen and Luce (2002) comment that some usability factors such as user preferences and satisfaction tend to be highly transient and specific, and therefore research on these issues need to focus on more stable characteristics of a given user community, such as 'the community's perspective on general document impact and the relationships between documents in a collection'.

Park (2000) comments that most earlier studies on the usability of multiple online databases have focused on technical and performance rather than interaction issues. Park's study shows that users prefer to interact with multiple databases through a common interface rather than an integrated interface because the former provides more control for the users on the selection of databases. Cultural issues have significant influence on the usability of digital libraries: Duncker, Theng and Mohd-Nasir (2000) comment that misinterpretation of the importance of colours, forms, symbols, metaphors and language for users coming from different cultural backgrounds can significantly affect the usability and user friendliness of digital libraries.

Bishop et al. (2000) comment that 'users don't know what they don't know, don't understand what they don't understand, and in any case, don't want to talk about it in a survey'. Hence researchers should be careful in choosing the method for studying the usability of digital libraries with end-users. Recent studies on usability testing with specific references to digital libraries include those of Blandford and Buchanan (2003), Allen (2002), Dickstein and Mills (2000) and Mitchell (1999). Usability issues of e-books have been widely studied and reported on by Wilson and Landoni (see for example, Wilson and Landoni, 2003; Wilson, Landoni and Gibb, 2003; and Wilson, Shortreed and Landoni, 2004).

Usability testing: methods and criteria

Several methods and guidelines have been proposed for conducting usability tests (see for example, Rubin, 1994; Kling and Elliott, 1994; Dumas and Redish, 1993). Blandford and Buchanan (2003) list the various usability factors that apply to the digital libraries:

- achieving goals: how effectively and efficiently users can achieve their goals with a system
- learnability: how easily users can learn to use the system
- help and error recovery: how well the system helps users avoid making errors, or recover from errors
- user experience: how much users enjoy working with the system
- context: how well the system fits within the context in which it is used.

A closer look at the above usability factors reveals that while some of the parameters are related to technical and systems design issues, others are related to the users. The following is a set of general guidelines and parameters that may be used to measure the usability of information services providing access to scholarly information sources.

Interface features

The user interface is the point of contact between an information service and the user, so it has a significant impact on the usability of the entire system. Every feature of the interface, ranging from the look and feel to the design, colour, fonts and facilities, will affect usability. More specifically one needs to check:

- the types of interface; for example, simple or novice vs expert or advanced
- the language of the interface, including options for using more than one language for display of the options, query formulation, and so on
- choices for navigation, shortcuts and easy movement among the various options and screens
- screen features including the use of colours, typography, layout and graphics
- options for personalization; for example, choice of a particular design, choice for the selection of channels of information, number of records per page, sort options, display options, and so on.

Search process

Broadly speaking, three major processes are involved in an information search session: database selection, query formulation and result manipulation. Each information service provides different options for each of these processes, and each option influences the usability of the system, as described below.

Database selection

This function is relevant to the systems that provide access to more than one database. It is important to note whether the system allows the users to choose one or more databases for searching, how easy it is to select a database, and how quickly one can revert to another database.

Query formulation

This is the most difficult and also the most important stage in an information search process. Each information service provider uses a specific set of options for the formulation and modification of queries. A number of parameters may be noted including:

- the search options – basic and advanced
- the mode of query formulation: form, natural language search, command mode, and so on
- options for formulating complex queries involving more than one search term or phrase and search operators
- search fields:
  - fields that can be searched
  - formulation of queries including the use of search operators, truncation and using multiple values in a single search field
  - options for marking a multi-word term as a phrase
  - options for searching in text and other databases (images, multimedia, and so on)
  - tools available to support search term selection, for example indexes and thesauri (especially for subject search), and guidelines for their use
- multiple database or resource search:
  - possibility of using a single search query when searching multiple databases or resources
  - existence of a common search interface for searching various channels
- query modification and saving:
  - options for modifying a query

— creation of search sets and conducting searches on a previously retrieved set of results

— options for saving one or more queries for future reference.

Result manipulation

It is important to note the various options available for display and manipulation of search results, including the following:

- formats available for the display of search results and individual records
- limits on the number of records that can be displayed – default vs user options
- options for navigation in the list of records
- marking of the records for display and saving
- options for sorting results
- separate display for the output from each chosen channel or database
- options for printing, exporting and e-mailing of records
- options for filtering duplicate records.

Help

Different kinds of help may be available for the various stages of an information search process, and in each case it is important to note its:

- appropriateness for the target users
- usability, including the language, style and context
- consistency of terminology, design and layout
- correctness.

It is also important to note whether error messages are displayed and, if so, whether the system also displays the measures for corrections, if necessary.

Usability of hybrid libraries: user problems and possible solutions

Academic users are probably the largest and the most frequent users of digital library services. Most university libraries today are hybrid libraries in the sense that they provide access to a range of printed and digital information resources. University students, staff and researchers can now access a variety of digital resources ranging from e-journals and e-books to electronic databases, local and remote digital libraries and the world wide web. However, it is important to know how easily users can get access to all the information resources relevant to their queries. A simple usability study was conducted towards the end of 2003 with a typical hybrid library website of a university in Scotland. Fifty-five students from the MSc Information and Library Studies class were chosen for this study. Each student was asked to choose a topic of research, and was asked to use the university library website to find information resources relevant to the topic. There were 55 topics. The following examples show the kind of research topics chosen by the users:

* marketing public library services
* intellectual property laws in Britain
* the Harry Potter book series: its impact on library readership and protests from religious groups
* e-government: implementing electronic elections and democracy
* digital libraries and their use
* managing digital libraries
* the influence of the horror genre on modern cinema
* privacy and ethics in an electronic age.

In order to make the searches realistic, no restrictions were imposed on the users regarding search time, and the choice of the type of information resources and/or services available through the library web pages. The users were asked to find all the possible resources relevant to their query, including book materials (which could be found through the library OPAC); journal and conference papers, which could be found through a number of e-journals and electronic databases; theses and dissertations, which could be searched through the university thesis collection; and all other types of resources that could be accessed through the websites or search tools with links from the library webpage. Users were asked to stop when they considered that a reasonable number of resources of all the different types were found. While searching for information using a specific system such as e-journals or electronic databases, users could stop when they thought that enough time had been spent on it, even if the desired results were not obtained. Thus, the objective was not to compare the performance of the users or of one or more specific channels providing access to electronic information resources, but to measure the overall usability of digital (strictly speaking hybrid) libraries. Users were asked to note down their experience, especially the level of difficulties faced while conducting the searches, and were asked to comment on each search system and the overall digital library.

User problems and related issues

Overall, a qualitative approach was adopted for this research, in that the users were given freedom to describe their difficulties and comments. Each user noted a number of difficulties faced in the course of the search process. While these were not always the same, and the wording of comments was sometimes different, some common issues and problems influencing usability were identified. Some of the most important findings of this study obtained from users' comments are summarized below.

1   Users felt that a search for electronic information resources calls for some basic ICT and information literacy skills without which a search may never be fruitful.
2   Users found that sometimes initial searches did not produce any good hits, yet there may be a wealth of information resources that are relevant to a search topic.
3   A particular search may produce too many or too few hits. Therefore users should be prepared to spend time to try out the various alternative search options.
4   Different systems – online search service providers, e-journals and aggregators, web search tools and digital libraries – have different

search interfaces and often use different search syntax; this makes the learning curve very steep.

5 Familiarity with the search topic and the structure of the digital library as well as the organization and content of the various systems – e-journals, online databases, digital libraries, and so on – helps the user produce better search results with relatively less time and effort.

6 There may be a number of e-journals and databases covering a given subject. It is often difficult for the user to decide which journal or database to select, and yet this is the first step and it determines the choice of the appropriate search service provider (for electronic databases) or aggregator (for e-journals).

7 Searches through online databases, e-journals, and so on often produce only abstracts, and the user has to go through another course of action to get access to the full text of the retrieved items.

8 Some search options such as 'keyword', 'subject', 'title keyword' and 'subject keyword' are often confusing; users generally found it difficult to differentiate between them.

9 Off-campus searching is often very time-consuming and frustrating, because the low bandwidth connection from home computers can result in a search and download taking a long time, and while the search is carried out the connection is sometimes broken. On many occasions the user is prompted to enter the password to re-establish the connection. This is frustrating for the user.

10 Sometimes a search produces too many hits and the user has to spend a lot of time (for example for full text journal articles) to decide whether or not an item is relevant.

11 A significant amount of useful information is available on the departmental and faculty intranet sites in the form of lecture notes and handouts, useful reading materials and pre-prints, suggested websites and digital resources, and it would be useful if this material could be linked to the library web pages.

12 Organization of information on the main library page has an impact on the user's selection of a specific digital library service; sometimes the specific services are hidden under several layers, and the user may have to explore the library web page to discover the various resources and services available.

13 Given the variety of information resources obtained as output, it is often difficult to decide which one to use; to determine the most relevant items retrieved is a challenging task.

14 Once the user chooses to search on a specific service, such as an electronic database, it is difficult to come back to the library web page and start another search. Results from the first search need to be saved, and then the user has to come back to the library web page and choose another system to search, often going through the whole process (log-in procedures) again.

15 Selection of appropriate search terms is a big challenge, especially for a complex or unfamiliar topic, and yet this is the first step in any search.

Possible solutions

The above findings highlight some of the most common problems faced by today's digital library users. Several design and user issues are involved here. Possible design measures are suggested below in reference to the various problems mentioned above. It may be noted that in order to resolve some problems, more than one measure must be taken. Overall, these measures may improve the access and usability of digital information resources.

- Point 1: This has direct implications on digital and information literacy training; indeed regular digital and information literacy training is not adequate in most cases, and yet the complexities of the digital information environment call for regular and rigorous training being provided.
- Points 2, 3 and 4: These suggest that users should be prepared to spend more time searching for information, in contrast with the typical web search duration of two to three minutes (Chowdhury, 2004). This has to be stressed in any user education or information literacy training; it is also an important design consideration.
- Point 4: A one-stop window approach where the user can see and use only one search interface to search information from a variety of systems may resolve this problem.

- Point 4: A task-based information access system may resolve this problem; alternatively there should be enough online help to guide the user.
- Points 5, 6, 7 and 8: These have implications for information literacy, user education and online help facilities.
- Point 9: This is directly related to the digital divide. Most recent statistics show only whether a household has an internet connection or not. However, in order to make it worthwhile to access and use digital libraries, it is important to have a high bandwidth connection.
- Point 10: This is an important point since web search studies reported earlier in this paper noted that users do not spend much time looking at their search output. Automatic filtration mechanisms based on user characteristics, user tasks and user choices may be useful.
- Points 11 and 12: A task-based information access system may be designed to provide access to the library as well as the institutional intranet and internet resources.
- Points 12, 13 and 14: Cross-database searching facilities with options for discarding duplicates and ranking the results (based on user-driven criteria) may resolve the problem.
- Point 15: Facilities for using search term dictionary or vocabulary control tools are essential for good digital library search interfaces.

Interoperability of various information access systems

One of the major issues with digital information is interoperability, an attribute which ensures that a wide variety of computing systems can work together and/or talk to one another. There are different types of interoperability, such as systems interoperability, software interoperability or portability, semantic interoperability, linguistic interoperability, and so on. Since the introduction of computers in creating catalogues, libraries have faced interoperability problems, and several tools and standards have been produced to help them, including the standardization of cataloguing (for example Anglo-American Cataloguing Rules), bibliographic formats (standard formats such as MARC21, UNIMARC and CCF), data exchange formats (international standards such as ISO 2709) and information retrieval (standards such as ANSI Z39.50).

Interoperability among various information access systems can be achieved in a number of ways, for example by adopting:

* common user interfaces
* uniform naming and identification systems
* standard formats for information resources
* standard metadata formats
* standard network protocols
* standard information retrieval protocols
* standard measures for authentication and security, and so on (Arms, 2000, 70–2; HyLife, 2002).

The Open Archives Initiative (n.d.), supported by the Digital Library Federation, develops and promotes interoperability standards that aim to facilitate the efficient dissemination of the content of publicly available e-print archives. The Open Archives Initiative Protocol for Metadata Harvesting (n.d.), referred to as the OAI-PMH, is an application-independent interoperability framework, which provides a mechanism for harvesting XML-formatted metadata from repositories.

Conclusion

While web and digital libraries have opened up many new opportunities for end-users to access scholarly information resources, they have brought many new concerns related to access to and usability of these services. As discussed in this chapter, the HCI community has taken a narrower view of usability when related to the user interfaces of information systems. Information science researchers, however, have a taken a wider view. The general parameters for assessing the usability of information services, proposed in this chapter, take into consideration the various stages in an information search process.

Despite many technological developments and growth in the variety and number of information access channels, users still find it difficult to use information services. The small survey reported in this chapter provides a list of at least some of the major problems facing users of digital libraries. Many of these problems may be resolved by taking some design measures as suggested here. Nevertheless, parallel to the developments in the web and digital libraries, continuous research on the use and usability of electronic information resources and services should be carried out in order to meet the overall objective of all this research – to make information usable with the least possible cost and effort. After all, this is the guiding principle of information services: to facilitate access to the right information at the right time at the least cost.

References

Allen, M. (2002) A Case Study of the Usability Testing of the University of South Florida's Virtual Library Interface Design, *Online Information Review*, **26** (1), 40–53.

Arms, W. (2000) *Digital Libraries*, Cambridge MA, The MIT Press.

Bishop, A. P, Neumann, L. J., Star, S. L., Merkel, C., Ignacio, E. and Sandusky, R. J. (2000) Digital Libraries: situating use in changing information infrastructure, *Journal of the American Society for Information Science*, **51** (4), 394–413.

Blandford, A. and Buchanan, G. (2003) Usability of Digital Libraries: a source of creative tensions with technical developments, *TCDL Bulletin*, www.ieee-tcdl.org/Bulletin/current/blandford/blandford.html [accessed 20 April 2004].

Bollen, J. and Luce, R. (2002) Evaluation of Digital Library Impact and User Communities by Analysis of Usage Patterns, *D-Lib Magazine*, **8** (6), www.dlib.org/dlib/june02/bollen/06bollen.html.

Borgman, C. (2000) *From Gutenberg to the Global Information Infrastructure: access to information in the networked world*, New York, ACM Press.

Brinck, T., Gergle, D. and Wood, S. (2001) *Usability for the Web: designing websites that work*, San Francisco, Morgan Kaufman.

Byerley, S. and Chambers, M. B. (2002) Accessibility and Usability of Web-based Library Databases for Non-Visual Users, *Library Hi Tech*, **20** (2), 169–78.

Choudhury, S., Hobbs, B. and Lorie, M. (2002) A framework for Evaluating Digital Library Services, *D-Lib Magazine*, **8** (7/8), www.dlib.org/dlib/july02/choudhury/07choudhury.html.

Chowdhury, G. G. (2004) *Introduction to Modern Information Retrieval*, 2nd edn,

London, Facet Publishing.

Dickstein, R. and Mills, V. (2000) Usability Testing at the University of Arizona Library: how to let the users in on the design, *Information Technology and Libraries*, **19** (3), 144–51.

Dumas, J. S. and Redish, J. C. (1993) *A Practical Guide to Usability Testing*, Norwood NJ, Ablex.

Duncker, E., Theng, Y. L. and Mohd-Nasir, N. (2000) Cultural Usability in Digital Libraries, *Bulletin of the American Society for Information Science*, **26** (4), 21–2.

Hansen, P. (1998) Evaluations of IR User Interface: implications for user interface design, *Human IT: Tildskrift för studier av IT ur ett humanvetenskapligt perspektiv*, **2**, www.hb.se/bhs/ith/2-98/ph.htm [accessed 29 May 2004].

Hearst, M. (1999) User Interfaces and Visualization. In Baeza-Yates, R. and Ribeiro-Neto, B. (eds), *Modern Information Retrieval*, New York, ACM Press, 257–323.

Hert, C. A., Jacob, E. K. and Dawson, P. (2000) A Usability Assessment of Online Indexing Structures in the Networked Environment, *Journal of the American Society for Information Science*, **51** (11), 971–88.

Hilbert, D. M. and Redmiles, D. F. (2000) Extracting Usability Information from User Interface Events, *ACM Computing Surveys*, **32** (4), 384–421.

Human-Computer Interaction Lab (n.d.) Improving Usability in Information Services: user interface evaluation metrics and new widgets, www.cs.umd.edu/hcil/pubs/UMDWLib.shtml [accessed 25 May 2004].

HyLife (2002) The Hybrid Library Toolkit: interoperability, http://hylife.unn.ac.uk/toolkit/Interoperability.html.

Kling, R. and Elliott, M. (1994) Digital Library Design for Usability, www.csdl.tamu.edu/DL94/paper/kling.html [accessed 20 April 2004].

Marchionini, G. (1992) Interfaces for End-user Information Seeking, *Journal of the American Society for Information Science*, **43** (2), 156–63.

Marchionini, G. and Komlodi, A. (1998) Design of Interfaces for Information Seeking. In Williams, M. E. (ed.), *Annual Review of Information Science and Technology*, **33**, Medford NJ, Learned Information, 89–130.

Mitchell, S. (1999) Interface Design Considerations in Libraries. In Stern, D. (ed.), *Digital Libraries: philosophies, technical design considerations, and example scenarios*, New York, Haworth Press, 131–81.

Nielsen, J. (1993) *Usability Engineering*, Boston, Academic Press.

Norlin, E. (2000) Reference Evaluation: a three-step approach — surveys, unobtrusive observations, and focus groups, *College & Research Libraries*, **61** (6), 546–53.

Open Archives Initiative (n.d.) www.openarchives.org/documents/index.html [accessed 26 May 2004].

Open Archives Initiative Protocol for Metadata Harvesting (n.d.) Version 2.0 of 2002-06-14. Document Version 2003/02/21T00:00:00Z, www.openarchives.org/OAI/2.0/openarchivesprotocol.htm [accessed 26 May 2004].

Palmer, J. W. (2002) Web Site Usability, Design, and Performance Metrics, *Information Systems Research*, **13** (2), 151–68.

Park, S. (2000) Usability, User Preferences, Effectiveness, and User Behaviours when Searching Individual and Integrated Full-Text Databases: implications for digital libraries, *Journal of the American Society for Information Science*, **51** (5), 456–68.

Rubin, J. (1994) *Handbook of Usability Testing: how to plan, design and conduct effective tests*, New York, John Wiley & Sons.

Savage-Knepshield, P. A. and Belkin, N. J. (1999) Interaction in Information Retrieval: trends over time, *Journal of the American Society for Information Science*, **50** (12), 1067–82.

Shneiderman, B. (1998) *Designing the User Interface: strategies for effective human-computer interaction*, 3rd edn, Reading MA, Addison-Wesley.

Shneiderman, B., Byrd, D. and Croft, W. B. (1997) Clarifying Search: a user-interface framework for text searches, *D-lib Magazine*, **3** (1), www.dlib.org/dlib/january97/retrieval/01shneiderman.html.

Shneiderman, B., Byrd, D. and Croft, W. B. (1998) Sorting out Searching: a user-interface framework for text searches, *Communications of the ACM*, **41** (4), 95–8.

Van House, N., Butler, M. H., Ogle, V. and Schiff, L. (1996) User-centred Iterative Design for Digital Libraries: the Cypress experience, *D-Lib Magazine*, www.dlib.org/dlib/february96/02vanhouse.html.

White, M. (2002) Information Architecture and Usability, *EContent*, **25** (4), 46–7.

Wilson, R. and Landoni, M. (2003) Evaluating the Usability of Portable Electronic Books. In *Proceedings of the 2003 ACM Symposium on Applied*

Computing (SAC), March 9-12, 2003, Melbourne, FL, USA, ACM, New York, ACM Press, 564–8.

Wilson, R., Landoni, M. and Gibb, F. (2003) The WEB Book Experiments in Electronic Textbook Design, Journal of Documentation, 59 (4), 454–77.

Wilson, R., Shortreed, J. and Landoni, M. (2004) A Study into the Usability of e-Encyclopaedias. In Haddad, H., Omicini, A., Wainwright, R. L. and Liebrock, L. M. (eds) *Proceedings of the 2004 ACM Symposium on Applied Computing (SAC), Nicosia, Cyprus, March 14-17, 2004*, New York, ACM Press, 1688–92.

6

The next information revolution: how open access will transform scholarly communications

David C. Prosser

Introduction

The birth of modern scholarly communications can be dated to the second half of the 17th century with the launch of the *Journal des Savants* in 1665 and the *Philosophical Transactions of the Royal Society* in 1666. At this time scientists (although they would not have used the term to describe themselves!) were driven by two motives to publish – they wanted to communicate their discoveries and share knowledge, but they also wanted to lay intellectual claim to their discoveries and insights, so registering intellectual priority. In the 300 years that followed authors continued to feel the force of these drivers. As researchers increasingly had to compete for research grants and university positions their publication records became the main features of their CVs. Journals, therefore, had a ready supply of 'raw material'.

Journals also easily found readers. Researchers need to keep up with the latest results and the scholarly literature became a research tool as new discoveries were built upon the work of others described within journals. Quality was assured through the system of independent peer review and libraries ensured the continuing availability of historical research by maintaining archives.

The number of researchers, the amount of research published, and the number of journals has grown steadily since 1665, until in the second half of the 20th century the system began to show signed of severe strain. Libraries could no longer afford to purchase all the journals that all the researchers at their institutions required. This led to declining subscriptions followed by increased prices as publishers tried to maintain their profit margins. Prices increased more rapidly than library budgets thus leading to more cancellations and further price increases, triggering a vicious cycle of reduced access to research. This is the well documented 'serials crisis' (a collection of papers on this topic can be found at www.lib.utk.edu/~jon/crisis.html).

The internet

The introduction of the internet in the 1990s brought a number of changes to the way that the literature is accessed and used. Firstly, in many cases it has accelerated the transfer of knowledge. In some subject areas electronic pre-prints make results available months earlier than they would have been in the old, print-only system. Even in subject areas where pre-prints are not the norm, online publication makes papers available to all subscribers at the same time as it eliminates postal delays. More fundamentally, reading patterns have changed as readers can now access the literature from their desks, rather than having to go to the library. This is probably also promoting a shift towards searching for information (through online abstracting services) rather than browsing (through journal tables of content).

The internet has also allowed libraries to come together to purchase information as consortia and for publishers to offer their entire corpus of journals for sale as bundles. In this way, average researchers now have access to more of the literature than they did ten years ago. While this is obviously a good situation it is not destined to last for long. The rate of increase in the costs of providing access to these electronic bundles continues to be higher than the rate of increase in library budgets. Therefore, we will see the same pattern as has been observed over the past 30 years – the number of people with electronic access will slowly decline as the price of access increases.

This is where the Scholarly Publishing and Academic Resources Coalition (SPARC) comes in. The rise of the internet and new digital publishing technology gives us the opportunity to examine carefully what it is that libraries, researchers and scholars require of a scholarly communications system. In particular, SPARC has begun to think of new tools and business models that better provide the international dissemination and impact that authors require, together with quality control and access needed by readers. The combination of institutional repositories and open access journals is increasingly being seen as giving libraries and researchers their first chance to change fundamentally the way that scientific information is communicated. They hold out the promise of providing a fairer, more equitable, and more efficient system of scholarly communication, one that can better serve the international research community.

The situation today

Many thousands of words have been written on the serials crisis and its cause. Basically, it represents a gap between the proportion of the literature that libraries can access and the information that researchers need in order to be effective. This gap has widened as over the last few decades the annual rise in average subscription price for science, technical, and medical (STM) journals has outstripped the increase in library budgets around the world. For example, the Association of Research Libraries (2003) report that the average cost of STM journals rose by 227% between 1986 and 2002, while the US consumer price index rose by 64%. During this period, spending on journals by ARL libraries managed to keep pace with the price rises, but only by transferring an ever increasing proportion of the library budget to journals. Not all institutions worldwide, especially those institutions that are less well funded than the ARL members, have been able to keep up with price rises.

SPARC

ARL members founded SPARC in 1998 in order to change scholarly communication's status quo. This was followed in 2002 with the launch of SPARC Europe to further the agenda of SPARC in Europe. Today, SPARC is an alliance of universities, research libraries and organizations (205 members in North America, Asia and Australia, and 69 members in Europe) that responds constructively to market dysfunctions in the scholarly communication system. Worldwide, SPARC helps expand information dissemination and use in a networked digital environment while responding to the needs of academe.

SPARC believes that two key conditions are necessary for fundamental change to occur in scholarly communication: scholars and scientists must recognize the benefits of change, and mechanisms for recovering the costs must be implemented. SPARC addresses both of these requirements, linking broad advocacy of change with real world demonstrations of how new models of scholarly communication might actually work.

SPARC advances its strategy via a range of activities:

1 Education programmes aimed at enhancing public and stakeholder awareness of scholarly communication issues and the promise of open access.
2 Advocacy of fundamental changes in the system and culture of scholarly communication. This encompasses outreach to various stakeholder groups in order to build support for expanded institutional and scholarly community roles in and control over the scholarly communication process.
3 Incubation of alternative publishing ventures and initiatives. SPARC reduces the risk faced by alternative publications and models via publisher partnership programmes that marshal library support of innovative new journal publishing programmes and business planning services that help non-profit ventures organize for sustainability.

SPARC has been able to demonstrate new models of scholarly communication through its partnership programme. Partner journals and partner projects (in the fields of science, technology, and medicine and the social sciences) undergo a rigorous screening process and meet strict criteria before SPARC encourages its member libraries to consider subscribing. SPARC partners support ventures that demonstrate open access or otherwise innovative business models; support development of non-profit portals that serve the needs of a discrete scientific community by aggregating peer-reviewed research and other content; and support lower cost, directly competitive journals as an alternative for academic disciplines formerly dependent on high priced journals.

Current SPARC partners include:

- BioMed Central
- BioOne
- Directory of Open Access Journals
- Economics Bulletin
- Evolutionary Ecology Research
- IEEE Sensors Journal
- Journal of the European Economic Association
- MIT CogNet
- Neuro-Oncology
- Organic Letters
- Public Library of Science
- Theory and Practice of Logic Programming

This is a partial list; for a complete list of partners see SPARC (2004).

A seismic shift

SPARC partner journals, like most leading peer-reviewed journals, are available online. Online publishing, beneficial in many ways for publishers, readers, and libraries, presents a particular quandary for libraries, which do the actual purchasing for their institutions. To wit: libraries have over the past few years taken advantage of consortia and bundle deals to access more material than they had subscribed to in print. In online publishing, there are few additional costs in allowing extra libraries to subscribe to online journals (once the initial costs of publishing online have been covered). Therefore, a library can be offered online access to all of a publisher's titles, rather than print access to a proportion of the titles. Alternatively, libraries can band together in consortia to negotiate a deal whereby all members of the consortium gain access to all journals in the publisher's portfolio. Invariably, these deals are priced by the publisher at a rate above what the library (or consortium) currently spends with that publisher.

There are undoubted benefits to institutions in taking up these deals as they are able to extend greatly the amount of material they can offer to their researchers. However, to find the extra money for the bundles the library often has to cut back in other areas – this can mean cancelling journals that are not part of large bundles (for example, high quality journals from society publishers). Further, the annual rate of increase in price for the bundles is often much in excess of any increase in library budget. This is especially true currently when many libraries around the world are actually facing budget cuts. To maintain the bundles, libraries must transfer additional funds from the monograph acquisitions budget or cancel journals that are not part of the bundles. So, having initially gained access to additional titles, we now face a new serials crisis where the librarian does not even have the freedom to cancel under-used journals that are part of the bundle.

(A further crisis – the 'permission crisis' – has been identified by Peter Suber (2003a), whereby legal and technological barriers limit how libraries may use the journals for which they have paid. These barriers are made up of copyright law, licensing agreements and management of digital rights that block access.)

The information gap described above has resulted in widespread dissatisfaction with the current scholarly communication model at a number of levels. Authors want to put their work before their peers and before society as a whole, and they do this without any expectation of direct financial reward, for example from royalties. In fact, they often have to make a financial contribution to the costs of publication in the form of page charges, figure reproduction charges, reprint costs, and so on, as well as giving away the copyright in their text, thus limiting their further use of their own work. In return for donating their papers (together with a financial contribution and surrender of copyright), the current system places barriers between authors' work and their potential readers, so resulting in reduced dissemination and impact of their work.

Readers are dissatisfied as they cannot get access to all the research that they need. The research literature is the most potent research tool available – it educates, provokes and inspires researchers. The current system denies access to the complete body of the literature, making the tool much less powerful and reducing the effectiveness of researchers. Librarians are dissatisfied as they are not able to meet the information needs of their users (both researchers and students). Even the wealthiest institutions cannot purchase access to all the information that its researchers require. In 2003 a UK report accepted that 'providing all of the information required by UK researchers is beyond the capability of any single library; and indeed that the aggregated efforts of all UK research libraries are failing to secure a national collection in keeping with the researchers' current and emerging needs and demands' (Research Support Libraries Group, 2003).

Finally, society as a whole loses if we continue with sub-optimal communications channels that restrict the free flow of information between the world's scholars and the public.

New opportunities

As a result of the problems described above, many organizations, including SPARC, have looked at the continued development of the internet and new electronic publishing tools and have asked whether it might be possible to re-engineer totally the scholarly communication process. Rather than only producing online versions of print journals accessed using traditional subscription-based models, might there be new financial models that use new technology to better fulfil the functions of journals and better serve authors, readers and, ultimately, research?

The most profitable approach to finding ways of using new technology and business models to provide solutions to the serials crisis is to look carefully at what it is that journals actually do. Traditionally, journals have been seen to perform four functions – registration, certification, awareness and archiving (Roosendaal and Geurts, 1998):

- registration – the author wishes to ensure that they are acknowledged as the person who carried out a specific piece of research and made a specific discovery
- certification – through the process of peer review it is determined that the author's claims are reasonable
- awareness – the research is communicated to the author's peer group
- archiving – the research is retained for posterity.

The traditional journal integrated all these functions into the print issue, distributed through subscriptions. This made perfect sense in the print environment where the production of extra copies incurred extra costs, which were recovered by charging subscriptions. In the new environment dominated by the internet and digital publishing technologies it is perhaps no longer the case that integrating these functions is the most efficient solution.

In December 2001 a meeting was convened in Budapest to address these issues, to scrutinize potential new models, and to investigate the best ways in which the new technology could be used. As a result of this meeting the Budapest Open Access Initiative (BOAI) was published in February 2002 (www.soros.org/openaccess). The BOAI identified two parallel and complementary strategies that could be used to move towards a fairer, more equitable and more efficient communications system. These were self-archiving and open access journals.

Self-archiving refers to the right of scholars to deposit their refereed journal articles in searchable and free electronic archives. Those providing open access journals do not charge for access to the papers, but make the papers available to all electronically and look to other financial models to cover the costs of peer review and publishing. They do not invoke copyright or exclusive licences to restrict access to the papers published within them; rather they encourage the dissemination of research limited only by the reach and extent of the internet. These complementary approaches will now be investigated in more detail to show how by acting together they can fulfil the functions required of a 'journal'.

Self-archiving in institutional repositories

The terms 'institutional repositories' and 'open archives' have been used to describe digital collections capturing and preserving the intellectual output of a single or multi-university community (Crow, 2002). They may contain a wide range of materials that reflect the intellectual wealth of an institution – for example, pre-prints and working papers, published articles, enduring teaching materials, student theses, data sets, and so on. The repositories would be cumulative and perpetual, ensuring ongoing access to material within them. By building the archives to common international technical standards – specifically, to the Open Archive Initiative (OAI) standards (for details of institutional repository technical specifications see the Open Archive Initiative at www.openarchives.org) – the material deposited within them will be fully searchable and retrievable, with search engines treating the separate archives as one. Readers will not need to know which archives exist or where they are located in order to find and make use of their contents. To maximize the use and impact of the repositories the material within them should be available freely over the internet.

While an institutional repository can make available a wide range of material (as described above), this paper is concerned only with the peer-reviewed research literature. If researchers were to place the results of their research into their local institutional repository – to self-archive their papers – three of the functions of a traditional journal would be immediately met:

1 Registration – by depositing in the repository the researcher would make claim to their discovery.
2 Awareness – by constructing the repository to OAI standards the institution would ensure that the researcher's work would be found by search engines and available to their peers. New alerting services could be developed that would inform readers of new papers deposited in any repository that matched their research interests (in the same way that journal tables of content can be received).
3 Archiving – the institution would be responsible for maintaining the long term archive of all the work produced by members of that

institution. This would place the onus of archiving back onto the library community where it has rested for centuries, rather than on the publisher community where it has migrated following the transfer from print to online. In many cases the research library will be best placed to maintain over many decades an archive of its own research.

As well as fulfilling these three functions of the traditional journal, there are many benefits, at many levels, to institutional repositories:

* for the individual they:
  — provide a central archive of the researcher's work
  — increase the dissemination and impact of the individual's research because they are free and open
  — act as a full CV for the researcher
* for the institution they:
  — increase the institution's visibility and prestige by bringing together the full range and extent of that institution's research interests
  — act as an advertisement for the institution to funding sources, potential new researchers and students, and so on
* for society they:
  — provide access to the world's research
  — ensure long term preservation of institutes' academic output
  — can accommodate increased volume of research output (no page limits, can accept large data-sets, 'null-results', and so on).

Peer review and open access journals

The one function of the traditional journal that self-archiving in institutional repositories does not fulfil is certification or peer review. Each institution will be able to make its own policies on how material is to be deposited in the repository, and some may insist that papers receive at least an initial review before being made widely available. However, this will not be a substitute for independent, international peer review. Peer review serves readers as a mark of quality (helping them to decide which papers they wish to read), while it is used by authors to validate their research (which is of particular importance in their next grant proposal or attempt at promotion).

Peer review journals could sit comfortably with the network of institutional repositories. Authors who wanted their work to be peer-reviewed could, after they had deposited it in their local repository, send it to their journal of choice. At this stage the work would be evaluated as in the current system and, if considered by the editor of the journal to be acceptable, the paper would be published in the journal and so receive the journal's quality stamp. The authors could then place a peer-reviewed 'post-print' onto their local institutional repository ensuring that both versions were archived.

Obviously, with all the relevant material available for free on a network of institutional repositories it becomes impossible for a journal to charge a subscriber to access a paper in the journal. The peer review journals, therefore, would need to have no access restrictions on them – that is, they would be 'open access'.

SPARC supports the open access movement via its advocacy and partnership activities; if implemented the movement would give free and unrestricted access through the internet to all primary literature published within the journal. This literature is given to the world by scholars without expectation of payment and in the hope that it is distributed and read as widely as possible. Making it freely available over the internet immediately distributes it to the 650 million people worldwide who have internet access. Giving all interested readers access will accelerate research, enrich education, share learning among rich and poor nations, and, ultimately, enhance return on investment in research (much of which comes from the world's taxpayers). From being in a position where institutions cannot supply all the information needs of researchers, researchers will be able to access all of the relevant information.

Open access repositories also provide major benefits for authors. Rather than their paper being seen by readers at the few hundred institutions lucky enough to have a subscription to the journal, the paper can now be seen by all interested readers. This increases the profile of the authors, their institutions, and their countries (see Suber, 2003a).

Without subscription income publishers will have to look at new financial models to support their journals. There are costs associated with the peer review process and with publication of a paper (even if it is only online), and these costs must be met somehow. A number of possible revenue sources for open access journals have been identified (Open Society Institute, n.d.), but one of the most stable for the science, technical and medical fields may be that where authors pay a publication charge, so ensuring that the publisher would receive sufficient revenue to make the paper available to all with no access restrictions. Ultimately, it would be for the funding body or the institution to cover the publication charge, but essentially this model looks to a move from paying for access to material (through subscriptions) to paying for dissemination.

Practical developments

The scenario above gives a vision for a fair and efficient mechanism for scholarly communications. All research material is made freely available in a worldwide network of fully searchable repositories. A sub-section of the material in the repositories – peer- reviewed papers – receives a certification 'quality stamp' from journals. This process is financed by the authors' institutions and funding bodies, rather than through the readers' libraries, allowing free access for all interested readers to all peer-reviewed papers via the internet.

This vision may sound utopian, but already many steps are being taken around the world to realize this future, and the pace of change appears to be increasing.

Institutional repositories

At least four open source software packages exist for setting up and implementing institutional repositories (GNU Eprints at http://software. eprints.org/, DSpace at www.dspace.org/, CDSWare at http://cdsware. cern.ch/ and Arno at www.uba.uva.nl/arno) and well over 100 institutions worldwide have used these packages to set up repositories. In addition, a number of national initiatives have been set up to provide infrastructure support for repositories – these include SHERPA in the UK (www.sherpa.ac.uk/), DARE in The Netherlands (www.surf.nl/en/themas/index2.php?oid=7), and the recent announcement of Australian $12

million to promote institutional repositories in Australia (www.dest.gov.
au/Ministers/Media/McGauran/2003/10/mcg002221003.asp).

As the amount of content in the growing number of repositories continues to increase, new services are being developed to make use of this
content. To date, the most active area of service provider development
has been the construction of search engines that can search over a number of repositories simultaneously, ensuring that the reader can find
material irrespective of where it has been deposited (OAI, 2003). One of
these search engines, OAIster (http://oaister.umdl.umich.edu/o/
oaister/), now searches through over 3,000,000 electronic items in over
200 repositories.

Open access journals

The number of open access journals publishing high quality, peer-
reviewed research is growing. As described above, SPARC and SPARC
Europe are in partnership with a number of these journals (SPARC,
2004), in particular BioMedCentral, which has now published over 4500
open access papers in 100 journals. Lund University has compiled the
Directory of Open Access Journals (DOAJ, www.doaj.org) listing fully
peer-reviewed journals that place no financial barriers between the
papers published online and readers. The DOAJ was launched in May
2003 with 375 titles, a figure that has doubled to over 790 titles in less
than a year. One feature of the DOAJ is that records for each journal
listed can be easily downloaded by librarians and entered into their catalogues, thereby allowing readers to learn about the journals.

New open access initiatives are regularly being announced. In October
2003 the first issue of *PLoS Biology* was launched. Produced by the Public
Library of Science, *PLoS Biology* (www.plos.org) is the first in a proposed
stable of journal titles. It is aiming to publish the highest possible quality papers – rivalling such established titles as *Science* and *Nature*. The
first issue generated massive international publicity, with reports and edi-
torials in many of the world's leading newspapers. Like the
BioMedCentral titles, *PLoS Biology* is mainly financed through author
payments. The Public Library of Science plans to launch a *PLoS Medicine*
in late 2004.

In addition, a plan has been put forward to transform current subscription-based journals into open access journals (Prosser, 2003). Under this plan, authors are given a choice as to whether or not they are willing and able to pay a publication charge. If they are (and, of course, if the paper is judged acceptable for publication following peer review) the paper is made open access on publication. If they are unwilling or unable to pay the paper is only made available to subscribers. Over time, the proportion of authors willing to pay should increase and the publisher can begin to reduce the subscription price. Eventually, the entire journal will be open access.

This model has proved to be attractive to a number of publishers, especially smaller and society publishers who believe in the moral case for open access but who did not see a way of converting their journals. The model means that authors who pay receive the benefits of open access (wider dissemination, more citations, greater kudos, and so on), while allowing those authors who do not pay the opportunity still to publish in their journal of choice. As the benefits of open access become clear (and in this hybrid model they can be accurately measured) authors will place pressure on their funding bodies to provide grants for publication.

While not eliminating financial risk for the journal owner, this model does reduce the risk by providing a smooth transition period as the decline in subscription revenue is matched to the increase in publication revenue. It is probably for this reason that a number of 'traditional' publishers such as Oxford University Press (www3.oup.co.uk/nar/special/14/default.html), the Company of Biologists (www.biologists.com/openaccess.html) and the American Physiological Society (www.the-aps.org/publications/pg/interest.htm) are experimenting with variations of this model.

Support from funding bodies

In 2003 there was increasing support for open access (in the form of self-archiving and open access journals) from the funding bodies that pay for research. In April 2003 a meeting organized by the Howard Hughes Medical Institute resulted in the Bethesda Declaration (available at www.earlham.edu/~peters/fos/bethesda.htm). This was followed by a statement of strong support for open access by the Wellcome Trust in the UK (www.wellcome.ac.uk/en/1/awtvispolpub.html). In October, all the major German funding bodies signed the Berlin Declaration supporting open access (www.zim.mpg.de/openaccess-berlin/berlindeclaration. html). The Berlin Declaration has also been adopted by, among others, the CNRS and INSERM in France, the FWF Der Wissenschaftsfonds in Austria, and the Fonds voor Wetenschappelijk Onderzoek in Belgium. This support from the funding bodies has come about as they realize that, to quote the Berlin Declaration, 'Our mission of disseminating knowledge is only half complete if the information is not made widely and readily available to society.' Funding bodies increasingly believe that it is in their interests and it is their responsibility to support the wider dissemination through open access of the research results that they have funded.

Interest in open access is also increasing at the political level. In December 2003 the UK House of Commons Science and Technology Committee announced an inquiry into scientific publications. The stated scope of the inquiry was to look 'at access to journals within the scientific community, with particular reference to price and availability' and to ask 'what measures are being taken in government, the publishing industry and academic institutions to ensure that researchers, teachers and students have access to the publications they need in order to carry out their work effectively'. Written evidence from interested parties (publishers, learned societies, libraries, academics, and so on) was invited in early 2004 and oral evidence heard in March and April 2004. The announcement of the inquiry is at www.parliament.uk/parliamentary_ committees/science_ and_technology_committee/scitech111203a.cfm, while transcripts of the oral sessions are at www.publications.parliament.uk/pa/cm/cmsctech. htm. The report of the Committee is being eagerly awaited within the UK and beyond as its recommendations may have a significant impact on the future scholarly communications environment.

The power of open access

As open access is a relatively new concept, it is difficult to compare directly open access publication (either through self-archiving or in peer-reviewed journals) with closed, subscription-based access. However, initial evidence is accumulating that supports the intuitively obvious assertion that open access will give greater dissemination and impact.

Recent figures from the *Astrophysical Journal* show that for 72% of papers published, free versions of the papers are also available (mainly through ArXiv). Greg Schwarz' citation analysis shows that these 72% of papers are, on average, cited twice as often as the remaining 28% where there are no free versions available (in Stevens-Rayburn, 2003). At this stage it is difficult to show clear cause and effect, but it is an intriguing indication of the increase in impact of authors' work if they self-archive.

The difference in the number of downloads between closed, subscription-based journals and open access journals is even more dramatic. Working from Elsevier's 2003 half-year results, Peter Suber (2003b) calculated that the average number of downloads for articles in ScienceDirect over the past year was 28. Over the same period the average number of downloads for articles in BioMedCentral was 2,500. This would suggest that publication in an open access journal gives, on average, 89 times as much usage as publication in a subscription-based access!

There are a number of reasons why this may not be an entirely accurate comparison, but Elsevier have refused to give the average downloads for biomedical papers published over the past year and so a direct comparison cannot be made. But even if 89 times is an over-estimate, it is clear that the evidence is beginning to show that open access does give greater dissemination, usage and impact, and as authors become more aware of this they are increasingly going to want to publish in open access journals and to deposit their papers in their local institutional repositories.

Next steps

There is growing international momentum in favour of institutional repositories and open access journals. Increasing numbers of libraries are taking on the role of hosts for institutional repositories, becoming responsible for maintaining the intellectual heritage of their institutions.

The libraries are also increasingly resisting the old models of subscriptions and bundling. Growing numbers of open access journals are attracting high profile editors and quality papers from excellent authors. These papers are viewed by more and more readers, increasing the impact and visibility of the journals. In addition, the continued success of these open access journals is proving the feasibility of the new business models.

As issues surrounding institutional repositories and open access journals become more widely discussed there is increasing awareness among authors of their need to retain their publishing rights (for example, does assigning copyright mean that they cannot put a copy of their own paper on their departmental website?). There is also increasing awareness among editors and editorial board members of their power and responsibilities to engage their publishers in discussions about fairer publishing practices. As described above, the past year in particular has seen a burgeoning of interest internationally in publishing issues amongst funding bodies and at the political level.

As success is evident, more authors, readers, university administrators, librarians and funding bodies are becoming aware of the limitations of the current system and the possibilities of the new models. More importantly, they wish to take positive action to bring about a change in the system as quickly as possible. Over the next few years all players in the communication process can play a part in making change happen. In particular, authors can:

- deposit their work in institutional repositories
- support open access journals by submitting papers to them and refereeing, reading and citing articles in them
- launch new open access journals if appropriate
- discuss publication rights, open access and reasonable prices with the publishers of the journals they use regularly (especially if they are editors or board members)
- discuss with funding bodies and university administrators funding and promotion criteria to ensure that researchers are not penalized for using repositories or publishing in open access journals (especially those that are online only)

- lobby funding bodies for specific publication funds to take advantage of the benefits of publishing in open access journals.

Librarians can:

- establish institutional repositories
- help faculty archive their research papers (new and old) within the repository, digitizing older papers if necessary
- help open access journals launched at their institutions become known to other libraries, indexing services, potential funders and potential readers
- make sure scholars at their institutions know how to find open access journals and archives in their fields and set up tools to allow them to access them (for example by including the journals listed in the DOAJ in their catalogues)
- as open access journals proliferate, and as their usage and impact grow, cancel over-priced journals that do not measure up
- engage with university administrators and funding bodies to raise the issue of open access
- familiarize themselves with the issues (see, for example, Create Change at www.createchange.org)
- support SPARC and SPARC Europe at www.sparceurope.org to increase their efforts.

Conclusion

The text of the Budapest Open Access Initiative opened with the statement 'An old tradition and a new technology have converged to make possible an unprecedented public good.' We can see how by harnessing the power of the internet we can construct a system of scholarly communication that better serves authors (by giving them the wide dissemination they require) and readers (by removing access barriers to the information they need). This in turn will enhance research and education worldwide and bring great benefits to society.

Obviously, any attempt to change such a well embedded system with a high level of inertia will be difficult. However, the advantages of the new model are immense. By working together we have already made many great strides towards the new system and by continuing to work together we can achieve it. That is the aim of SPARC and SPARC Europe and of the many thousands of librarians, authors, readers, funders, publishers, and so on who see open access as the future of scholarly communications.

References

Association of Research Libraries (2003) Statistics and Measurement Program, www.arl.org/stats/arlstat/graphs/2002/2002t2.html.

Crow, R. (2002) The Case for Institutional Repositories: a SPARC position paper, www.arl.org/sparc/IR/ir.html.

Open Archives Initiative (2003) *Registered Service Providers*, www.openarchives.org/service/listproviders.html.

Open Society Institute (n.d.) Open Access Journal Business Guides, www.soros.org/openaccess/oajguides/index.shtml.

Prosser, D. C. (2003) From Here to There: a proposed mechanism for transforming journals from closed to open access, *Learned Publishing*, **16**, 163–6.

Research Support Libraries Group (2003) Final Report, www.rslg.ac.uk/.

Roosendaal, H. E. and Geurts, P. A. Th. M. (1998) Forces and Functions in Scientific Communication: an analysis of their interplay. In Karttunen, M., Holmlund, K. and Hilf, E. R. (eds) *Cooperative Research Information Systems in Physics Conference, CRISP 97, 31 August–4 September, Oldenburg, Germany*, www.physik.uni-oldenburg.de/conferences/crisp97/roosendaal.html.

Scholarly Publishing and Academic Resources Coalition (2004) *SPARC Partners*, www.arl.org/sparc/core/index.asp?page=c0.

Stevens-Rayburn, S. (2003) ASTRO: report from the AAS Publications Board meeting, message on PAMNET listserv, 13 November, http://listserv.nd.edu/cgi-bin/wa?A2=ind0311&L=pamnet&D=1&O=D&P=1632.

Suber, P. (2003a) Removing the Barriers to Research: an introduction to open access for librarians, www.earlham.edu/~peters/writing/acrl.htm.

Suber, P. (2003b) Posting to *Open Access News*, 5 September, www.earlham.edu/~peters/fos/2003_08_31_fosblogarchive.html#a1062763 32667919229.

7

Self-archiving publications

Stephen Pinfield

Introduction

The self-archiving of publications has the potential to revolutionize scholarly communication, making it more efficient and effective. But a great deal needs to be done before that potential can be realized. This chapter discusses some of the key issues associated with self-archiving. It analyses the ways in which self-archiving has so far developed, examines the possible benefits and drawbacks of self-archiving, and outlines the potential impact of the practice on scholarly communication.

'Self-archiving' (or 'author self-archiving' as it is sometimes known) is 'a broad term often applied to the electronic posting, without publisher mediation, of author-supplied research' (Crow, 2002, 11). The term was first used in the literature in 1999 by leading advocates of the practice, Stevan Harnad and Paul Ginsparg (for example, Harnad, 1999a, 1999b; Ginsparg, 1999a). It was used by them a year earlier in e-mail discussion lists (for example, Harnad, 1998). It seems they were (knowingly or unknowingly) adapting a term already in use among computer scientists meaning a program that archives files automatically. Ginsparg and Harnad were now applying the term to authors and their research papers.

What Harnad, Ginsparg and other proponents of self-archiving were (and still are) arguing is that authors of research papers should mount their work on the web so that all potential readers have free and unrestricted access to it. Such 'open access' to research literature would,

Harnad (2001a) suggests, ensure that it is 'freed' from the 'unwelcome impediment' caused by 'toll-gating access' in the form of conventional subscriptions, site licences and pay-per-view charges. Some practitioners have objected to the 'archiving' part of 'self-archiving' being used in this way to mean simply mounting a file on the web – the word implies to many a high degree of curation and preservation, which may not be present in the self-archiving scenarios discussed by Harnad. Nevertheless, the label has now been widely adopted within the information community and beyond.

History of self-archiving: arXiv

While the term 'self-archiving' may only have come into use in this field in 1998, the practice of self-archiving is much older than this. High energy physicists have been posting their papers in an open access repository since 1991. That was the year when arXiv, as it is now known, was set up at the Los Alamos laboratories by Paul Ginsparg and colleagues. Since then arXiv has become the most important vehicle for scholarly communication in high energy physics and related areas of mathematics and computer science. It now contains over 300,000 papers, is mirrored on several continents, and is widely used. It is hailed by its managers, now based at Cornell University, as an exemplar of effective open access web-based research communication.

ArXiv was originally designed to automate a pre-existing paper-based practice – the circulation of 'pre-prints'. Pre-prints are early versions of research papers before they have been refereed or formally published. Prior to the creation of arXiv, it was the practice of physicists to circulate hard copy pre-prints to colleagues in other research groups worldwide as a preliminary stage of scholarly communication. The circulation of pre-prints achieved three main objectives. Firstly, it was a way of establishing priority. Physicists (like most other researchers) are eager to lay claim to an idea if they first thought of it. Pre-prints were a way of registering that claim without having to wait for formal peer-reviewed publication. This leads to the second objective of pre-print circulation – rapid dissemination. Pre-print circulation, even in a paper-based world, was fast. It meant scientific progress itself (which involves building on the work of others) could also be fast. Thirdly, circulating a pre-print was a way of improving the finished article. Authors of pre-prints would often receive comments from colleagues, which could be incorporated in the final versions of papers submitted to peer-reviewed journals. This 'informal peer review', it was said, often led to better published papers.

Hard copy pre-print circulation had a major limitation. Regular circulation could only ever include a relatively small number of institutions, and so some researchers (at other institutions) would miss out. The Los Alamos archive was designed to address this problem. Instead of circulating paper copies, authors were able to FTP their papers to a central server. Others could then easily download the papers, thus making the research rapidly and widely available. With the advent of the web, this service became even easier to use for author and reader alike.

However, as with many things designed for a particular purpose, arXiv developed in unexpected ways. It was originally designed as a kind of 'bulletin board' to facilitate pre-print circulation; it was envisaged that pre-prints would be held for a temporary period only. However, it soon became clear that authors wanted it to be a long-term archive for papers. It also became clear that they wanted the repository to include not just pre-prints but also 'post-prints'. Post-prints are final versions of papers that have been revised in response to referees' comments and accepted for publication in journals. Electronic post-prints, of course, had a paper-based precedent. Authors would commonly circulate off-prints of their published papers, normally in response to a request from an interested colleague, albeit after the paper was formally published. The Los Alamos archive was seen as a convenient way of automating this and had the added benefit that the paper could be posted before it had appeared in the journal. It is common to see notes on papers in arXiv that the article has been accepted by and is forthcoming in a particular journal. It is clear then that arXiv has become a repository for electronic versions of papers both pre- and post-refereeing.

Electronic pre-prints and post-prints have become known collectively as 'e-prints', a term with a chequered history. Ginsparg (1999b) has described the history of the term. It was originally coined in the early 1990s by a mathematician, Greg Lawler, to describe electronic pre-prints. It was used more generally in the mid 1990s to mean 'electronic versions of anything'.

Ginsparg was, however, influential in redefining the word at that time to mean 'an article either in draft or final form SELF-ARCHIVED by the author' (original emphasis). This is the way the word is now generally used, particularly by users of arXiv, the largest e-print repository.

Brown (2001) and Pinfield (2001) have described how arXiv is currently used by physicists. The workflow is illustrated in Figure 7.1. The left hand column summarizes the well established process leading to publication in a peer-reviewed journal. This begins when an author writes a paper and submits it to a journal editor for consideration. The journal editor then sends the paper to one or more (usually two) referees who are working in the same field. The referees report back to the editor advising on whether or not the paper should be published. Assuming they recommend publication (as in Figure 7.1), they will normally suggest revisions to the paper. These suggestions are forwarded to the author, who is then expected to make the required changes. Following the submission of the revised version of the paper, it will be prepared by the publisher for publication with copy editing and formatting. Finally, it is published in an issue of the journal. The whole publication process can take 12 months, sometimes more. It extends beyond this, of course. The journal publisher or a secondary publisher will usually create metadata describing the paper, which may be incorporated into separately published finding aids.

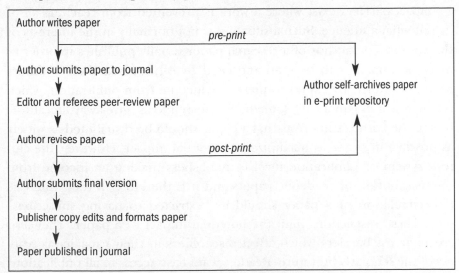

Figure 7.1   The journal publication process and self-archiving

Self-archiving in a repository such as arXiv commonly takes place at two points in the publication process, as Figure 7.1 shows. Firstly, before the paper is refereed, the author may post it on the e-print repository as a pre-print. Secondly, when the paper has been revised in response to referees' comments, the final version of the paper can be mounted on the repository as a post-print. The post-print is normally formatted by the author and so may not incorporate changes made by the publisher at the pre-publication stage. In fact arXiv does not normally accept publisher-produced files for copyright reasons (the publisher will normally own copyright in the layout of the formally published article). At each of these stages the author creates metadata describing the paper, which can be searched by users.

Benefits of self-archiving

A service such as arXiv creates benefits for the individual researcher and for the research community in general. The benefits stem from the fact that arXiv lowers barriers created by the conventional publication system. These barriers are often divided into two related categories: 'impact barriers' and 'access barriers' (see Harnad, 2001b). These labels perhaps need some further explanation.

Impact barriers exist where a work is prevented from reaching all of its potential audience. Such a situation is not normally in the interests of the author. The author of a research paper usually publishes in order to make an impact – to be read and cited by other researchers. Authors would not normally expect to make any income from publication, which is why research papers are sometimes referred to as 'give-away literature'. It is in the author's interests that a paper should be distributed as widely as possible in order to maximize its potential impact. However, the current system of publication involves publishers making an income from the distribution of academic papers and it is therefore in their interests that circulation of a paper should be restricted to paying subscribers only. These restrictions limit the potential impact of a paper. They also create access barriers which affect researchers in their capacity as readers of the scholarly literature. Readers want easy access to all publications in their field. However, the restrictions placed on access to the literature by publishers prevent this from happening. No academic institution can afford to subscribe to all peer-reviewed journals and so its members cannot gain easy access to all publications required for their research.

Benefits for the research community

Where these impact and access barriers are lowered for researchers by services such as arXiv, the benefits for the individual researcher soon become clear. The first and most obvious benefit is that papers are disseminated widely, thus maximizing their impact potential. Evidence is beginning to emerge that papers which are openly accessible are more likely to be cited (see for example Lawrence, 2001). A second benefit is that research is disseminated quickly. Formal publication in a peer-reviewed journal can take a year or longer. Even after a paper is accepted for publication in its final form there can be long delays until space can be found in the journal. Self-archiving, by contrast, is virtually instantaneous. A pre-print or post-print can be disseminated quickly by the author and can therefore have an immediate impact on research. For the reader, access is also quick and easy. The latest research literature is available in an unrestricted way from the desktop. Metadata describing papers can be searched and may even be pushed to registered users via e-mail alerts.

Benefits for individual researchers translate into benefits for the research community as a whole. The speed of dissemination means that scientific progress itself can be accelerated. Researchers have access to the latest results in their field. They can also be confident (and increasingly so as self-archiving on arXiv becomes widespread) that they have access to the full breadth of the research literature available. Better communication enables better science. An example of this might be that unintentional duplication of research can be avoided since scientists are more likely to be aware of each other's activities.

Such benefits would ostensibly carry over into other disciplines. Since the creation of arXiv, other similar services have been set up for separate subject communities. CogPrints for cognitive sciences, and RePEc for economics, are examples of these. Like arXiv both were set up by pioneering enthusiasts: Stevan Harnad in the case of CogPrints and Thomas

Krichel in the case of RePEc. They reflect the slightly different communication cultures of their disciplines but have in common that they both contain pre-refereed versions of papers as well as post-refereed. However, neither CogPrints nor RePEc has yet been as successful as arXiv. They do not contain as many full-text papers, nor have they achieved the same importance to researchers that arXiv clearly has to high energy physicists. The long-term success of each, of course, remains to be seen.

The development of other e-print repositories has prompted some of the supporters of self-archiving to speculate on the potential benefits of the practice were it to be adopted in a wide range of subject disciplines. The benefits of maximizing impact and access potential for individual researchers and the consequent benefits for their research communities would apply more widely. Scholarly communication as a whole would operate more efficiently and effectively. The benefits of this would be felt globally, not least in countries, such as in the developing world, where institutions currently find it difficult to afford access to more than a few peer-reviewed journals. Researchers in these countries would be better able to contribute to the ongoing development of scientific knowledge.

Benefits beyond the academic sector

Some have suggested the benefits would spread more widely still. There are wider social and economic benefits that might follow from making high quality research more easily available. Fundamental curiosity-driven research could more easily have an impact in applied areas. For example, there would be greater opportunities for knowledge transfer between the academic sector and the commercial sector. There would also be the potential for the public understanding of science to be enhanced. Science journalists and popular science writers would have better access to original research. Also, high school students could begin, with the guidance of a knowledgeable teacher, to become acquainted with the primary literature. The real weight of such arguments is difficult to assess at the present time, especially as the best example of self-archiving is currently in a discipline area (high energy physics), which is rather remote from commercial applicability and usually impenetrable to the uninitiated. Nevertheless, the attraction of making publicly funded research more easily available to the public is in principle a strong one. While such arguments are probably a long way from the original aims of the creators and users of arXiv, the benefits of self-archiving are potentially far-reaching.

Interoperability: the Open Archives Initiative

With a number of separate e-print repositories beginning to appear in the late 1990s, it became clear that their usefulness would be enhanced by the development of interoperability between them. The Open Archives Initiative (OAI) was set up in 1999 to provide this. The OAI 'develops and promotes interoperability standards that aim to facilitate the efficient dissemination of content'. The most important technical outcome of this initiative has been the OAI Protocol for Metadata Harvesting (OAI-PMH).

The OAI Protocol was designed as a way of transporting data. It facilitates an exchange of information between data providers and service providers. Data providers expose structured data (such as bibliographic records) on the internet so that it can be harvested by third parties. Service providers harvest the data (normally in the form of simple Dublin Core) from a number of different data providers, organize it and then make it available to users in various ways. They often make it available in a searchable form so that an end-user can carry out a search encompassing a large number of data providers by interacting with a single service provider system. In the real world, a service provider, such as ARC, harvests data (or strictly speaking metadata, which describes full-text papers) from a large number of OAI-compliant e-print repositories (and other similar services). The metadata is processed and presented to the end-user in a searchable form via a web interface. The end-user can search for e-prints held on a large number of different servers worldwide, by keywords from the title, abstract, subject terms or author names. If the user finds an item of interest, the record delivered by the service provider contains a clickable link to the full text of the paper held by the data provider. Tools are now available to ensure that OAI-compliant metadata can also be converted into HTML so that it can then be crawled by robots from mainstream web search engines, such as Google. This means that papers available in OAI-compliant e-print repositories are accessible to users not just via specialized OAI service providers but also via standard web search engine services.

The OAI Protocol is technically simple and this has facilitated widespread adoption. Since the release of version 2 of the Protocol in June 2002 (the experimental version 1 first came out in January 2001), it has been stable and can be implemented with confidence by information managers for production services. Many existing services, such as arXiv, were able to retrofit their systems to become OAI-compliant relatively quickly. New data providers can achieve OAI-compliance easily and cheaply, especially as there are now several pieces of free repository software, which come out of the box OAI-ready. Crow (2004) lists seven such software packages that are now available. The most established of these is the GNU e-prints (eprints.org) software, produced at the University of Southampton. This was originally based on the software used to deliver CogPrints. Pinfield, Gardner and MacColl (2002) have described the setting up of a GNU e-prints repository, which took about five person-days using an inexpensive server installation. The more recently released repository software from MIT and Hewlett Packard, DSpace, is now also being widely adopted. With the stabilization of the OAI Protocol and the release of free OAI-compliant software, the technical barriers for setting up an interoperable e-print repository have become very low.

The 'openness' of the Open Archives Initiative is strictly speaking a technical one. The OAI Protocol has introduced a technology for systemic openness allowing services to talk to each other. Nevertheless, the combination of open access and the OAI Protocol is a powerful one, which creates a number of benefits. The first benefit is enhanced accessibility. The content becomes more easily locatable and navigable for users. With repositories worldwide sharing interoperability standards there is the potential for a global virtual archive of research papers, entry into which can be gained from a single access point. The simplicity of the OAI Protocol (while a key to its success) does, however, create limits to interoperability. The Protocol deals in unqualified Dublin Core and this means the metadata from different data providers may be structured in different ways. As a consequence it is very difficult for service providers to, for example, create a meaningful browse index, since names or dates will be structured differently, and subjects will be described using different controlled vocabularies (or none at all). But despite this limitation the search tools created by existing service providers (such as ARC) are impressive.

Service providers can do more than just deliver search services. A second major benefit created by OAI is the potential for other developments, such as analysis of the literature. Key metrics, such as citation analysis of self-archived papers, can already be delivered. Citebase is an interesting example of this. The potential of such tools is enormous. They can create useful post-publication quality indicators, which could complement pre-publication quality assessment mechanisms such as peer review.

Institutional repositories

The centralized subject-based approach to self-archiving has not always been successful. Warr (2003) has described the low take-up of an experimental chemistry pre-print repository set up by Elsevier Science. While still up and running, this service has met with scepticism from most chemists, although Warr also reports on a limited amount of support and interest. In other subject disciplines, e-print repositories may not exist at all or may be no more than a 'pet project' of one or two enthusiasts. Some commentators have, however, seen latent demand for e-print repositories in many disciplines judging by the number of researchers who 'informally self-archive' their publications on their personal or departmental websites.

Since the majority of subject communities have not yet set up e-print repositories or adopted the practice of self-archiving on a significant scale, many supporters of self-archiving have come to favour an alternative strategy: institutional repositories. These are open access archives set up and run by organizations such as universities, which contain work by members of the institution. Institutions are ideally suited to support this kind of development for a number of reasons. Firstly, they have the resources to subsidize the start up of repositories and to fund their maintenance. Secondly, institutions have infrastructures (technical and organizational) to support them. Thirdly, institutions are able to provide a policy drive to encourage self-archiving among their members. Finally, it is argued, institutions have an interest in doing so. An institutional repository could potentially enhance the profile and prestige of an institution acting as an attractive shop window for research activities. A repository could also become part of a systematic information asset management initiative to be used in activities such as community outreach, media relations or accreditation management. There is also the potential benefit to the institution of long-term cost savings in periodical subscriptions if the literature becomes widely available on open access.

In some ways, then, the institutional approach to self-archiving is a pragmatic one. It is seen as a pragmatic way to try to encourage the wider adoption of self-archiving. Despite the fact, as it is sometimes commented, that researchers may identify more with their subject community than with their institution and would therefore be more inclined to self-archive in a subject-based repository, it is institutions that are more likely to foster self-archiving on a large scale. Nevertheless, with OAI functionality in place, the location of the full text of a paper (whether in an institutional or subject repository) is in fact largely irrelevant. If papers are self-archived on institutional servers, it is easy to imagine that subject communities may provide subject-specialist search provider views of the data.

It is possible, however, that institutions may use repositories in additional ways, in addition to facilitating the self-archiving of scholarly papers. Repositories may also be used to store other digital objects associated with research (or indeed teaching) activity. These could include image, audio and video files or data sets of various kinds. Lynch (2003) has described some of the potential. One simple development favoured by many researchers is that a published paper could be placed in a repository alongside the raw data produced during the research. The two could be linked in useful ways such that the communication of research results could be enhanced.

As well as providing immediate access to it, institutional repositories might also be used as a vehicle for preserving the scholarly output for the long term. This is a controversial idea among supporters of self-archiving. As Pinfield and James (2003) have described, some regard any concern with digital preservation to be a distraction from the central aim of encouraging self-archiving and achieving immediate access to the scholarly output. Harnad has argued this case (his views are outlined in Pinfield and James, 2003). On the other hand, some would say that preservation ought to be at the centre of the institutional repository mission. Crow (2002) described preservation as one of the key features that define an institutional repository. More work needs to be done in this area but there is clearly a potential to use repositories as a means of achieving the systematic preservation of digital objects of all sorts, including research papers.

Barriers to self-archiving

Despite the apparent benefits of self-archiving and the recent growth in support for the practice, significant barriers to its widespread adoption remain. The first barrier is lack of awareness. This is demonstrated by Swan and Brown (2004) who report on the results of a survey of authors sponsored by JISC and the Open Society Institute. Their respondents are divided into two groups: 'OA authors' (that is those who have published in open access journals) and 'non-OA authors' (those who have not). They report that 71% of OA authors and 77% of non-OA authors were not aware of any electronic repositories. This is a significant finding for supporters of self-archiving, which indicates that there is a major awareness-raising job to do.

Even where researchers are aware of repositories, there is still considerable inertia when it comes to self-archiving. Many are cautious about practising self-archiving and sceptical about its potential benefits. Their objections normally fall into four main categories: quality control (particularly peer review), intellectual property rights (particularly copyright), concern about disturbing the publishing status quo, and workload. These objections will be discussed in turn below along with possible immediate responses. A more detailed discussion of how the system of scholarly communication might develop when self-archiving is widespread will be reserved for the section on the future.

Quality control

Quality control is normally uppermost in the minds of researchers.

There is a common suspicion that self-archiving undermines peer review. Because e-print repositories distribute content independently of any formal peer review process they are often seen as a way of self-publishing without quality checks. There is a particular dislike of pre-prints in some disciplines. Of course, pre-prints are not a necessary part of an e-print repository. It is perfectly possible to set up a repository and only accept post-prints (or other documents which have been formally published or accepted for publication). Repositories are in themselves neutral with regard to quality control and so they can accommodate any form of quality assessment including peer review. The scenario advocated by most of the supporters of self-archiving – authors should submit their papers to peer-reviewed journals and also self-archive them – certainly takes into account the importance of peer review. Peer review is acknowledged to be important but it is recognized that at present it is carried out outside the e-print repository environment. In this case, repository managers should carry out low-level checks on quality before making a paper live on the system, but they can assume that the real quality checks occur elsewhere. Warr (2003) quotes Paul Ginsparg as describing this process for arXiv: 'We still think it's important to have a minimal level of screening, to keep the material at least "of refereeable quality", and avoid material that is manifestly irrelevant, offensive, or silly' (Warr, 2003, 367–8).

Under institutional management, e-print repositories could, however, be managed (if necessary) with higher levels of quality control. Self-archiving need not be the anarchic activity it is sometimes assumed to be (although some commentators would regard the supposed anarchy of self-archiving as a good thing). It is possible that schools or departments within the institution could have to give formal authorization before a paper is made live on the institutional server. Most repository software already has an authorization procedure built into the workflow. This could be implemented with a light or heavy touch depending on the preferences of stakeholders. There is no suggestion that this would replace peer review but rather that it could provide an additional first-line quality check which could screen out obviously inappropriate material.

Intellectual property rights

The second area of concern for many researchers is that of intellectual property rights and copyright. Most research institutions allow their employees to dispose of the copyright of their own papers as they (the authors) choose. Some journal publishers require authors to sign over exclusive rights before their papers are published. Publishers' policies do, however, vary (see Gadd, Oppenheim and Probets, 2003). Other publishers do not require exclusive rights to be transferred by the author and may even explicitly allow the posting of pre- or post-prints on the web. Authors need assistance at a local level in order to deal with the complexities of copyright. Most institutions have research support offices, which could expand to provide this sort of support. They could help to change the existing system where many authors are willing to sign almost anything put in front of them by publishers in order to get their paper published. Authors would then be supported in ways that would allow them to maximize the potential impact of their work without unnecessary restrictions.

Some authors have another concern in the area of intellectual property rights. They are concerned that their work is more likely to be plagiarized if they self-archive it on an open access server. There is, however, no empirical evidence to support this fear (although some publishers claim that they ask authors to sign over copyright in order to enable them to protect authors from plagiarism). It may be true that making material available online makes cut-and-paste plagiarism easier but this applies to all electronic information, not just that which is openly accessible. What can be said in favour of open access is that it makes detection of plagiarism easier. Many automatic plagiarism detection services can operate better when they can move around documents without barriers. For this reason, some have suggested that open access is actually more likely to discourage serious attempts at plagiarism. A determined plagiarist is most likely to choose a more obscure work to copy so that the dishonesty will not be noticed. In any case, it would be rather perverse of authors to prefer their work to remain in relative obscurity (limiting its potential impact) in order simply to guard against a hypothetical risk of plagiarism.

Concern about disturbing the publishing status quo

Perhaps the major barrier to widespread self-archiving is that authors just do not see the point. There are two related issues here. The first is the argument that the existing system of scholarly communication works, and that self-archiving will disrupt it without replacing it with anything workable. The second is that, whether the existing system works optimally or not, it is the reality within which researchers are required to work – all the reward mechanisms within their institutions and subject communities (promotion, peer recognition, and so on) are based on it, not on self-archiving. At best, self-archiving is an unnecessary distraction. At worst, it is a dangerous innovation, which has the potential to weaken the 'tried and tested' system.

The fear that self-archiving will fatally undermine the existing system is a common one but it does not seem to be borne out by the empirical evidence. The arXiv service has not destroyed journals. Journals are still valued by physicists for the quality certification function they perform. Taking this on board, most advocates of self-archiving support the idea that e-print repositories should complement rather than replace the existing system of peer-reviewed publication – at least in the short and medium-term. However, it is reasonable to expect that over time the character of journal publishing will alter if self-archiving becomes widespread. Publishers are likely to become managers of the peer review process (and perhaps providers of copy editing and formatting services) rather than distributors of content. However, this will probably happen gradually over a number of years and in the meantime self-archiving can proceed immediately. There is no immediate need for alternative business models to be in place. These will evolve naturally as practices change (their possible final shape is discussed in the section on the future, below).

Lack of personal incentive for authors to self-archive

Even if self-archiving is not likely to undermine the strengths of the existing system of scholarly communication, the fact remains that there is often little personal incentive for researchers to self-archive. Benefits of self-archiving apparent to physicists may seem rather remote from the concerns of other researchers and only seem to accrue if everybody does it rather than a few enthusiasts going their own way. Inertia rather than opposition is the biggest barrier to self-archiving at the moment. It needs to be taken seriously. Supporters of self-archiving are beginning to recognize that this can only be addressed by sustained advocacy within subject communities, institutions and other stakeholder organizations (including national and international agencies).

Another way of encouraging self-archiving is to put real support services in place to facilitate it. Making self-archiving as easy as possible for researchers will help to ensure that it is not just another administrative burden (the final, common objection to self-archiving). This has already been discussed in relation to legal advice on copyright but other services are also useful. Important among these is 'self-archiving by proxy'. Rather than expect authors themselves to self-archive (convert their files into acceptable formats, create the appropriate metadata, and deposit their work in the repository), institutional support services could offer to do this for them (if provided with the original file). Anecdotal evidence seems to indicate that such measures are going to be necessary if self-archiving is to enter the mainstream.

Self-archiving initiatives

In order to create some kind of momentum for the self-archiving movement, a number of initiatives have been set in motion in various countries. For example, in the UK, the FAIR programme has sponsored a series of development projects investigating (among other things) e-print repositories, e-theses services and associated intellectual property rights. Focus on Access to Institutional Resources (FAIR) is funded by the UK Higher Education Funding Council's Joint Information Systems Committee (JISC). The FAIR programme builds on previous JISC activities, such as the development of the GNU e-prints software. FAIR began in the summer of 2002, with a completion date of the end of 2005. It has funded a total of 14 different projects in UK universities which between them cost about £3 million (excluding institutional overheads). The programme was 'inspired by the vision of the Open Archives Initiative' and aimed 'to support the disclosure of institutional assets' (JISC, 2002).

Pinfield (2003) has described the main features of the programme and evaluative accounts of its progress will begin to emerge in 2005.

Similar programmes are underway in other countries. One of the first was the Mellon-funded programme in the USA. In the US, there is also the DSpace initiative, the California Digital Library eScholarship Repository and the Ohio State University Knowledge Bank. In the Netherlands, the Digital Academic Resources (DARE) programme is now up and running, and this has been followed in Germany by the Deutsche Initiative für Netzwerkinformation (DINI) initiative. In Canada, the Canadian Association of Research Libraries is sponsoring the Institutional Repositories Pilot Project, and in Australia, the Australian government is funding the Research Information Infrastructure Framework for Australian Higher Education programme. These different initiatives have slightly different aims and emphases but they are all attempting to address in practical ways some of the barriers to self-archiving outlined above and to kick start self-archiving in institutions and subject communities.

Many individual institutions also now have local initiatives in the area of self-archiving. These are often run by the library and information service but are beginning to capture the interest of researchers (albeit sometimes slowly). A few advocates of self-archiving have managed to secure institutional policy level backing. A good example of this is the Queensland University of Technology in Australia where there is now a policy in place which requires authors in the institution to self-archive their work in the institutional repository if the publisher copyright agreement permits it (Queensland University of Technology, 2003).

All of this is happening in a climate of greater interest in and support for open access. The first year when there were regular items on the scientific literature about open access issues, covering open access repositories and journals, was 2003. Scientific publishing in general and open access in particular also featured regularly in the financial, education and mainstream press. These news articles were partly generated by interest in the initiatives already mentioned. They were also a response to the increasing number of policy statements supporting open access launched during 2003. These included the Bethesda statement (2003, from US research funders), the Berlin Declaration (2003, from German funders), and the

Wellcome Trust statement (2003, from a leading funder in the UK).

The number of repositories and e-prints has grown rapidly since 2001 but is still relatively small. Mark Ware (2004) provided a snapshot of the field in January 2004. He identifies about 250 OAI data providers, 45 of which are institutional repositories. The median number of records in each repository was 314. For institutional repositories (excluding the CERN pre-print server), the mean number of documents per site was 1250 and the median number 290.

Unresolved issues

A number of significant unresolved issues remain in the field of self-archiving, some of the most important of which are discussed below. They include discipline differences, definitions of 'publication', versioning issues, digital preservation, costing and funding models and meta-data standards.

Discipline differences

The issue of discipline differences is perhaps the most important issue that requires further work. Will all disciplines naturally converge on a single model of communication based on e-print repositories? Ginsparg argues that this is the case:

> Regardless of how different research areas move into the future (perhaps by some parallel and ultimately convergent evolutionary paths), I strongly suspect that on the one- to two-decade time scale, serious research biologists will also have moved to some form of global unified archive system, without the current partitioning and access restrictions familiar from the paper medium, for the simple reason that it is the best way to communicate knowledge, and hence to create new knowledge. (Ginsparg, 1999a)

This optimistic view is, however, questioned by Kling and McKim (2000). They argue that different disciplines have developed different cultures of communication, and that those differences are likely to persist for the foreseeable future in the electronic era. They provide an account of the different practices that persist in different disciplines, which lead them to conclude that e-print repositories may not be universally adopted.

The question of whether certain disciplines are more inclined than others to accept self-archiving needs considerably more work. Some have observed that there appears to be a correlation between disciplines that have pre-existing pre-print cultures and those that have developed e-print repositories. It is, however, difficult to know how to read this. While an inclination to communicate informally through circulation of pre-peer reviewed research may explain early adoption of self-archiving, it may not necessarily be an indicator that other disciplines will not adopt e-print repositories in the medium or long term. Other disciplines may adopt self-archiving when it has become more formalized and will perhaps limit their postings to post-prints only. E-print repositories could be (and need to be) set up and managed in such a way that they can accommodate the variety of cultures of communication that exist in different subject communities.

Definitions of 'publication'

A related question is important here: does self-archiving a paper constitute publication? Stevan Harnad (2001b) argues forcibly that it does not. He defines 'publication' in a very particular way to mean the appearance of a paper in a peer-reviewed journal. Self-archiving a pre-print is therefore not publication. However, a number of journals have policies that they will not publish papers already made available on e-print repositories, regarding this as prior publication. The fact that the situation is ambiguous indicates that self-archiving is part of a trend in which the whole notion of publication is becoming more fluid. Publication may become more a process than a single event and the norms of such a process still need to be worked out.

Versioning

This leads to another issue: versioning. At present, peer-reviewed journals provide 'the version of record' – the definitive version of the author's work, which can be cited and archived. This version has normally been revised by the author following peer review, and copy edited and formatted by the publisher. In an open access e-print repository environment, what is the version of record? Post-prints are the final version of the paper produced by the author but have not been altered by the publisher. Does this matter? In the short term, researchers will probably need to continue to cite the article as published by the journal publisher (even if they initially access the paper via an open access repository). In the longer term, it is possible that papers held in repositories may become the version of record. Copy editing does not necessarily have to be carried out by publishers. It could be provided (if it is considered to be essential) as a stand-alone service to authors before the final version is deposited in an e-print repository. However, even in a situation where such arrangements are in place, versioning remains an issue. In an open access environment it is probable that many copies of the same paper may be made and then stored in different places (the 'many copy problem'). Suber (2004) has outlined the pros and cons of this phenomenon and has suggested ways in which the problems might be addressed. However, more work on this is certainly needed.

Digital preservation

In a system (still hypothetical) where the paper held in a repository becomes the version of record it will, of course, be necessary to ensure that version is preserved. Even before this, the issue of preservation of self-archived material is an important one. Pinfield and James (2003) have put forward arguments to support the case for the preservation of selected e-prints in the current situation. However, issues surrounding the costing, funding and management of preservation still need a great deal of further work.

Costing and funding models

Preservation is not the only activity associated with self-archiving where there needs to be more work on costing and funding models. In fact, the whole field of self-archiving requires further economic analysis and modelling. Barton and Walker (2003) have published some work on the costs of setting up and running an institutional repository, but these include a number of elements that do not necessarily have to be included in a simple e-print archive. On a larger scale, work needs to be done on the costs of a whole scholarly communication system that has open access e-print repositories at its centre. Apart from running the repositories, the main essential cost would be administering the peer review process (assuming that the hidden costs of author time and referee time continue to be covered in other ways). Traditional journals will continue to provide these services in the short term but if their subscription incomes fall as content becomes more easily available on open access, they would need to secure their income in different ways. It is possible that publishers could continue to provide quality control services but would perhaps need to secure their income at the input stage, charging for the peer-review process, rather than for subscriptions. In the long term, other stakeholders, such as learned societies or consortia of institutions, may provide peer review services on a cost recovery or even profit-making basis. The assumption is often made that e-print repositories are likely to result in cost savings for institutions since publishers would not be able to charge such high prices for content but this assumption requires further testing and analysis.

Metadata standards

At present, publishers (either the primary journal publishers or secondary publishers) generate metadata to enable article searching. The self-archiving process involves the creation of metadata, either by the author or a proxy. The structuring of that metadata is at present, however, very variable. More work needs to be done on the question of how this metadata could be standardized. Standardization could occur at data provider level, with data providers agreeing on detailed standards. Alternatively, it could occur at the service provider level, with post-harvesting normalization (or even enhancement) of metadata. Both create potential technical and organizational challenges, which need to be addressed.

The future of self-archiving

The future of self-archiving, particularly in relation to peer-reviewed journals, remains to be seen. If self-archiving is widely adopted in the way that its supporters expect, there will be both discontinuities and continuities with the existing system of scholarly communication. Free and unrestricted access to the research literature will be a revolutionary discontinuity. However, there will also need to be important continuities, the most significant of which is perhaps peer review. Scholarly communication needs robust quality control mechanisms. The majority of self-archiving advocates regard peer review as a given, which might be streamlined but should not be undermined. It remains to be seen whether some elements of the publishing system can be radically changed while at the same time leaving others intact.

The questions of what a new system with self-archiving at its centre would look like and how the transition might occur are important ones. Some have speculated on how the changes could unfold. Harnad cautiously suggests possible scenarios. Once the scholarly literature has been self-archived, he then suggests:

> One possible outcome is that that will be the end of it. The refereed literature will be free online for those who want it and cannot get it any other way, but those who can afford to get it the old way via paying journals will continue to do so. In this event, the access/impact problem will be solved . . .
>
> An alternative outcome is that when the refereed literature is accessible online for free, users will prefer the free version (as so many physicists already do). Journal revenues will then shrink and institutional savings grow, until journals eventually have to scale down to providing only the essentials (the quality-control service), with the rest (paper version, online PDF version, other 'added values') sold as options.   (Harnad, 2001a, 1025)

Harnad's account is intentionally sketchy. He does not attempt to go into any detail of what the economics of the system might be, for instance. Harnad has in fact always been reluctant to speculate in any detail on the long-term future, fearing that discussion on hypothetical scenarios may be a distraction from the immediate imperative to ensure the scientific literature is self-archived in the short term.

Others have not been so cautious. Crow (2002) describes a model where the different components of peer-reviewed journal publishing are disaggregated and could potentially be carried out by different parties. Simplifying this kind of analysis, it is clear that journals currently provide two essential features of scholarly publishing: peer review and distribution of content. In a new model, open access e-print repositories could become vehicles for the distribution of content. The issue of who would then provide peer review is a moot point. At present, peer review is carried out by researchers, overseen by an editor and editorial board under the umbrella of a journal. The same parties (expert researchers overseen by a group of senior academics) could continue to provide peer review with or without a journal title as an umbrella. Learned societies or consortia of institutions could form peer review groups to provide refereeing of papers outside the traditional journal environment. Papers in repositories would then be 'quality stamped' in some way to indicate to users that the work had undergone peer review.

Such a practice does not necessarily mean the end of journals. It does mean journals would be different. 'Overlay journals' may develop, where papers located in archives are selected and brought together in virtual journal issues. This process of selection could involve peer review. Smith (2000) has described how journals might transform themselves in order to coexist with e-print archives. Journals in this view can ' "overlay" what already exists, as opposed to communicating new, original content' (Smith, 2000, 47). They do, however, continue to provide peer review.

Peer review will remain a central feature of scholarly communication for the foreseeable future but other forms of quality assessment may also develop to complement it. At a pre-publication stage, as already discussed, institutional archives may put in place quality screening of various kinds before a paper is made live on the repository. Quality indicators may also be developed at the post-publication stage. If content is available on open access, counts of downloads and citations could be easily calculated at the article level for all the literature. Such metrics could be used to provide a post-publication assessment of the significance of a paper.

A system might develop then with several layers of quality control through which research output would pass, in response to which the content would potentially go through a number of iterations. There would be an initial quality screening before a paper was posted on a repository. This might prompt some changes to the paper. Following this, there would be a stage in which the author might receive comments from colleagues in the research field on the pre-print, and make any necessary changes. The paper would then be submitted for formal peer review. Changes would normally be expected at this stage. Mounting the post-print might generate further scholarly discussion and possible corrections, rebuttals or updates. The final stage of quality control, that of citation analysis and related metrics, would be less likely to produce changes in the article but would be likely to prompt further work. It would certainly help identify the key papers on which the subject community was building its ongoing work.

Guédon has described a multi-layered system like this. He argues that open access archives should be developed to incorporate quality certification mechanisms so that they can exist apart from traditional journals. He goes further, suggesting that widespread use of open access archives may even lead to the demise of the traditional scientific paper: 'In its place may gradually emerge a more fluid and flexible mode of scientific communication where a given individual could contribute as little or as much as he/she wants, so long as it is significant and accepted by his/her peers (Guédon, 2002, 12)'.

Scholarly communication would consist in an ongoing flow of information facilitated by interoperable open access repositories.

Conclusion

Guédon's vision may be some way off becoming reality even though the technology is already in place to achieve it. What needs to develop now are communication cultures and management frameworks that take advantage of the technical possibilities. Considerable progress has already been made, but a great deal remains to be done. Many institutions and other organizations have begun to implement practical repository initiatives. The next two to three years will tell us a great deal about whether or not a scholarly communication system based on e-print repositories will work. In the meantime, it is worthwhile to keep an eye on the big picture. The prospect of a scholarly communication system where academic authors can easily achieve the rapid and wide dissemination of their output and where readers can gain free and unrestricted access to the literature is worth pursuing.

Acknowledgements

Thanks to Bill Hubbard for his useful comments on drafts of this paper.

References

Barton, M. R. and Walker, J. H. (2003) Building a Business Plan for Dspace, MIT Libraries' Digital Institutional Repository, *Journal of Digital Information*, **4** (2), http://jodi.ecs.soton.ac.uk/Articles/v04/i02/Barton/.

Berlin Declaration (2003) *Berlin Declaration on Open Access to Knowledge in the Sciences and Humanities*, Max-Planck-Gesellschaft, www.zim.mpg.de/openaccess-berlin/berlindeclaration.html.

Bethesda statement (2003) www.biomedcentral.com/openaccess/bethesda/.

Brown, C. (2001) The E-volution of Pre-prints in the Scholarly Communication of Physicists and Astronomers, *Journal of the American Society for Information Science and Technology*, **52** (3), 187–200.

Crow, R. (2002) *The Case for Institutional Repositories: a SPARC position paper*, Washington DC, SPARC. Release 1.0., www.arl.org/sparc/IR/ir.html.

Crow, R. (2004) *A Guide to Institutional Repository Software*, 2nd edn, New York, Open Society Institute, www.soros.org/openaccess/software/.

Gadd, E., Oppenheim, C. and Probets, S. (2003) RoMEO Studies 1: the impact of copyright ownership on academic author self-archiving, *Journal of Documentation*, **59** (3), 243–77, (e-print) www.lboro.ac.uk/departments/ls/disresearch/romeo/RoMEO%20Studies%201.pdf.

Ginsparg, P. (1999a) Journals Online: PubMed Central and beyond, *HMSBeagle*, 3–16, www.biomednet.com/hmsbeagle/61/viewpts/page5.

Ginsparg, P. (1999b) Re: The Significance of the LANL Preprint Server, AmSci Forum Email Discussion List, 23 July, www.ecs.soton.ac.uk/~harnad/Hypermail/Amsci/0347.html.

Guédon, J.-C. (2002) Open Access Archives: from scientific plutocracy to the republic of science, *Proceedings of the 68th IFLA Council and General Conference, August 18–24, 2002* , www.ifla.org/IV/ifla68/papers/guedon.pdf.

Harnad, S. (1998) Re: Savings from Converting to On-Line-Only: 30%– or 70%+ ?, AmSci Forum Email Discussion List, 31 August, www.ecs.soton.ac.uk/~harnad/Hypermail/Amsci/0052.html.

Harnad, S. (1999a) Advancing Science by Self-Archiving Refereed Research, *Science dEbates* 31 July, www.sciencemag.org/cgi/eletters/285/5425/197#EL12.

Harnad, S. (1999b) Free at Last: the future of peer-reviewed journals, *D-Lib Magazine*, **5** (12), www.dlib.org/dlib/december99/12harnad.html.

Harnad, S. (2001a) The Self-archiving Initiative, *Nature*, **410** (26 April), 1024–5, and *Nature: webdebates*, www.nature.com/nature/debates/e-access/Articles/harnad.html.

Harnad, S. (2001b) For Whom the Gate Tolls? How and why to free the refereed research literature online through author/institution self-archiving, now, www.cogsci.soton.ac.uk/~harnad/Tp/resolution.htm.

JISC (2002) *Circular 1/02: Focus on Access to Institutional Resources Programme (FAIR)*, Bristol, Joint Information Systems Committee, www.jisc.ac.uk/index.cfm?name=circular_1_02.

Kling, R. and McKim, G. (2000) Not Just a Matter of Time: field differences and the shaping of electronic media in supporting scientific communication, *Journal of the American Society for Information Science*, **51** (14), 1306–20, (e-print), http://arxiv.org/abs/cs.CY/9909008.

Lawrence, S. (2001) Free Online Availability Substantially Increases a Paper's Impact, *Nature*, **411** (31 May), 521, and *Nature: webdebates*, www.nature.com/nature/debates/e-access/Articles/lawrence.html.

Lynch, C. A. (2003) Institutional Repositories: essential infrastructure for scholarship in the digital age, *ARL Bimonthly Report*, (226), www.arl.org/newsltr/226/ir.html.

Pinfield, S. (2001) How Do Physicists Use an E-Print Archive? Implications for institutional e-print services, *D-Lib Magazine*, **7** (12), www.dlib.org/dlib/december01/pinfield/12pinfield.html.

Pinfield, S. (2003) Open Archives and UK institutions: an overview, *D-Lib*

Magazine, **9** (3), www.dlib.org/dlib/march03/pinfield/03pinfield.html.

Pinfield, S., Gardner, M. and MacColl, J. (2002) Setting up an Institutional E-Print Archive, *Ariadne*, **31** (March–April), www.ariadne.ac.uk/issue31/eprint-archives/.

Pinfield, S. and James, H. (2003) The Digital Preservation of E-prints, *D-Lib Magazine*, **9** (9), www.dlib.org/dlib/september03/pinfield/09pinfield.html.

Queensland University of Technology (2003) *Policy F/1.3 E-print repository for research output at QUT*, Brisbane, www.qut.edu.au/admin/mopp/F/F_01_03.html.

Smith, A. P. (2000) The Journal as an Overlay on Preprint Databases, *Learned Publishing*, **13** (1) 43–8, www.ingentaselect.com/alpsp/09531513/v13n1/contp1-1.htm.

Suber, P. (2004) The Many-Copy Problem and the Many-Copy Solution, *Open Access Now*, **14** (15 March), www.biomedcentral.com/openaccess/archive/?page=features&issue=14.

Swan, A. P. and Brown, S. N. (2004) *JISC/OSI Journal Authors Survey: report*, Truro, Key Perspectives Ltd., www.jisc.ac.uk/uploaded_documents/ACF655.pdf.

Ware, M. (2004) *Publisher and Library/Learning Solutions (PALS): Pathfinder research on web-based repositories: final report*, Bristol, Mark Ware Consulting Ltd, www.palsgroup.org.uk.

Warr, W. A. (2003) Evaluation of an Experimental Chemistry Pre-Print Server, *Journal of Chemical Information and Computer Sciences*, **43**, 362–73.

Wellcome Trust (2003) *Scientific Publishing: a position statement by the Wellcome Trust in support of open access publishing*, London, www.wellcome.ac.uk/en/1/awtvispolpub.html.

Websites

ARC
  http://arc.cs.odu.edu/
arXiv
  http://uk.arxiv.org/
California Digital Library eScholarship Repository
  http://escholarship.cdlib.org/

CERN Scientific Information Service
  http://cds.cern.ch/
Chemistry Preprint Server
  www.chemweb.com/preprint
Citebase
  http://citebase.eprints.org/cgi-bin/search
CogPrints
  http://cogprints.ecs.soton.ac.uk/
DARE
  www.darenet.nl/en/toon
DINI
  www.dini.de/dini/arbeitsgruppe/arbeitsgruppe_details.php?ID=9
DSpace
  www.dspace.org/
eprints.org (GNU eprints)
  www.eprints.org/
FAIR
  www.jisc.ac.uk/index.cfm?name=programme_fair
Institutional Repositories Pilot Project (Canada)
  www.carl-abrc.ca/projects/ir/
JISC
  www.jisc.ac.uk
Ohio State University Knowledge Bank
  https://dspace.lib.ohio-state.edu/index.jsp
Open Archives Initiative
  www.openarchives.org
Open Society Institute
  www.soros.org/
RePEc
  http://repec.org/

MODELS AND ECONOMICS OF SCHOLARLY PUBLISHING

8

Electronic books

Louise Edwards

Introduction

For the last 500 years, printed books have proved to be the ideal tool for scholars to communicate with their audience. Whether from peer to peer, tutor to student or perhaps establishing a dialogue with the wider public, the book is the channel by which knowledge and ideas are passed from author to reader and from one generation to the next. As such, it performs a critical cultural, educational and social role. At the beginning of our new millennium, the printed book faces a new challenge in the form of electronic media. This chapter presents an overview of where technology might take us in our relationship to the book.

The context

The book as we know it today is a product of technological progress, and the process of scholarship follows closely in its wake. The backdrop to change is the shifting social, political and economic environment. Kilgour (1998) traces the evolution of the form of the book and concludes that several concurrent elements were necessary to its development. Within the context of constant human learning and discovery, society has always had a considerable need for information and knowledge transfer. As technology advanced, the printed book was the most effective means of sharing information that could being integrated successfully into existing systems *and* was also economically viable.

Johns (1998) highlights the value-added properties held within the modern book, which we perhaps too readily take for granted. We *trust* the reliability of the information it contains. We rely on the authenticity of the author. We know we are likely to be reading one of many distributed copies, all looking exactly the same and with a clear stated purpose. Because the production of printed material is based on a set of principles set down over the years, we all readily understand the structure of the book, from its title page, to its chapters and sub-chapters. These are all features of the 'print culture'. The key elements of this print culture are, according to Eisenstein, in her seminal work (1979), those of standardization, dissemination and fixity. Eisenstein demonstrated how the process of scholarly communication, so familiar to us today, was able to develop as a result of the invention of printing. The printing press made possible new forms of structuring and presenting information to help the reader and, as a result, changed the nature of scholarly communication, allowing modern methods of scholarship to emerge. Cataloguing, indexing, pagination and other features helped people discover the existence of individual titles and provided ways for the reader to find their way around the text itself. Printing facilitated the production of multiple standardized versions of a work and, as Landow (1997) points out, multiple copies of a fixed text permitted readers in different times and places to consult and refer to the 'same' text. It therefore gave scholars much easier access to texts, allowing development of the relationship between them, as well as between the teacher and the taught. The economics of book production led to the development of copyright, based around concepts of creativity and originality. Printed materials changed approaches to thinking and of problem solving; new patterns of reading emerging from the way content was presented on a page. Printing played an important part in the establishment of an archival process, storing knowledge produced by many different people within a single format.

Printing influenced methods of measurement and of data collection. Olson (1994) shows how the press, by placing an 'original' copy of a text, which was basically free from copying errors, into the hands of scholars who could study and comment on it, facilitated the emergence of the modern research tradition. The impact on both mind and society were profound: 'our modern conception of the world and our modern conception of ourselves are, we may say, by-products of the invention of a world on paper' (Olson, 1994). In essence, print affected the way that knowledge of all kinds came into being and was distributed and, as such, it affected all aspects of political, social and cultural life.

The emergence of the electronic book

Our thinking about the electronic book is shaped, by and large, by what we know well – the paradigm of the printed text: 'we so tend to take print and print-based culture for granted that, as the jargon has it, we have "naturalized" the book by assuming that habits of minds and manners of working associated with it have naturally and inevitably always existed' (Landow, 1997). However, the emergence of the electronic book presents a potential challenge to our well-established notions of fixity, standardization and methods of dissemination. As Feather (2003) says, 'at the beginning of the 21st century, systems of communication are undergoing profound change'.

The context for such change is clear. Media and communication systems are undergoing a process of convergence, inevitably altering patterns of information distribution and of structure. The impact for all players in the information chain, from author, to publisher, to reader, is significant, as the relationships between them will inevitably change. Feather presents a circular model of relationships between players, which he clusters into 'knowledge creators', 'knowledge distributors' and 'knowledge users', see Figure 8.1.

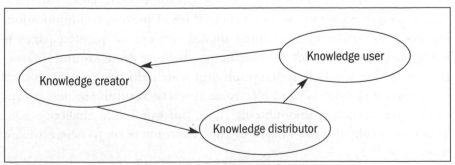

Figure 8.1   Publishing: an interactive model (Feather, 2003)

Kist (1987) defines communication as the process of social exchange, and information as the object of an exchange between 'supplier' and 'user'. 'Process' is the means by which such information is handled and transmitted, and 'format' describes the form in which the content is made available to the user. Using these terms, he suggests that people within the communication chain, which may include authors, publishers and readers, will be able to interact and exchange knowledge and information freely with each other, as active participants, as part of a dynamic, circular relationship rather than by a linear process. Knowledge banks created by the players in the chain will also be dynamic. Landow (1997) promises readers a world of 'multilinearity, nodes, links and networks', offering them multiple paths through knowledge, blurring the boundaries between reader and author, teacher and student: 'just as printed books did, hypertext systems are dramatically changing the role of students, teacher, assignment, evaluation, reading list, and relations amongst instructors, courses, departments and disciplines'. Suddenly, the limitations of the printed book begin to become clearer:

> Structurally, the printed book is a medium that operates as a monologue, isolating producer and reader. Feedback and interaction are extremely limited, demand elaborate procedures, and only in the rarest cases lead to corrections. Once an edition has been printed it cannot be corrected; at best it can be pulped.　　　　(Enzensberger, 1970)

This brings us back to our consideration of the role and performance of the book as a primary object for the communication of knowledge and ideas. Lynch (2001), in his major article on the e-book, poses the question as to our expectations about the nature of human communication. He asserts that simply presenting digital versions of printed pages is inadequate and that a lot of thinking needs to be done around the successors to the scholarly monograph and instructional materials, which capitalize on the potential of electronic delivery, resulting in new genres of material. Lynch is undoubtedly right, but our initial challenge is to understand fully the road taken by the electronic book to where we are now.

E-book publishing: the last decade

Charting the development of the e-book industry provides a complex and interesting mix of the traditional and the new. Many powerful players entered the industry, not least Microsoft and Adobe, while some of the fledgling e-book businesses did not survive the dot.com revolution. The 1990s were a period of rapid expansion, fuelled by considerable venture capital spent on digitization and fast growth of new workforces in fresh enterprises, mostly based in the United States and with an emphasis on content for the US market. Forecasts for growth at that time were wildly optimistic. The sudden tightening of the capital markets forced many e-book companies to contract and resulted in the casualties of the dot.com bubble. It had been built on the assumption that consumers would want a large electronic library and would be prepared to pay for it. The lesson learnt was that, too frequently, the content was not right, the reading experience was unsatisfactory and the business model unattractive.

It was largely the new enterprises that received their share of press coverage but, quietly, the major publishers were gearing up for electronic book publishing. Taylor & Francis made a move as long ago as 2001, when it announced that it was to digitize its whole academic backlist of 15,000 titles. Many academic publishers followed a policy of producing new academic titles in electronic formats, along with selective digitization of out-of-print titles.

The 'e-book experience'

On the face of it, the e-books we have today appear to offer scholars a number of advantages. Full-text search capabilities and linking to other resources are powerful features. The reader is also in control of the way the material is presented; for example, each reader can alter font and character size to suit their requirements. Convention may be to have a larger font size for the chapter heading than for the running text, but with e-books, the reader will decide for themselves. Many e-books have study tools incorporated within them, giving the user the ability to underline, highlight and annotate text.

However, the technological advances to date have produced an electronic reading device that simply does not match that delivered by the printed text. Early e-book equipment was slow, clumsy and expensive. It did not connect to the internet and was limited in the range of applications it could handle. Devices varied in sophistication, weight, portability and memory and storage capacities, but probably the most serious disadvantage has been the quality of the visual display:

> the format of the electronic book in no way resembles that of the convenient codex that has been traditional for nearly the last two thousand years, and it has met with unenthusiastic reception, chiefly because it presents a radical physical change for the user: from the familiar bound book in the hand to the monitor screen of a desktop computer or the flat-panel display of a laptop machine.   (Kilgour, 1998)

The physical attributes of the book currently win out over the computer screen. In short, the current technology is not yet sufficiently mature. Kilgour pinpoints two main factors needed to persuade the market to adopt electronic books in large numbers – the device that delivers content, and the content itself. The optimal reading device will be easier to use than the printed book, will give an exceptional quality of display, will be highly portable and realistically priced. It will deliver a wide range of content that can be tailored to the user's needs and is constantly updated – in essence, a personal library. It will also offer communication facilities, creating a forum for discussion and dialogue. The expectations are that the hand-held device market *will* definitely develop but the need is for a multi-purpose device and for much improved screen technology.

At the time of writing, the technology appears to be changing fast. Sony and Philips are launching electronic book devices with a display that mimics paper and can be read inside or outside. Philips and the E-Ink Corporation have jointly developed a new display, which looks like paper and can be read at any angle and in any light. Are we getting somewhere near the much-promised 'electronic paper'? What will such technology mean for the development of the monograph and the textbook?

What does the market want?

Market research undertaken by Armstrong and Lonsdale (2003), on behalf of the Joint Information Systems Committee in the UK, aimed to investigate the perceptions and attitudes of information professionals towards electronic books. It targeted specific subjects in higher education where there is both demand and available content, including medicine, business and engineering, and also involved a mix of staff within further education colleges. Publishers were very much involved in the project, participating in focus groups and debating the findings, in order that the whole information chain could work together on understanding user needs. The opinions of the stakeholder groups were found to be extremely positive in general, with e-books showing potential to address several strategic and operational issues in academic institutions. E-books were regarded as a major cornerstone for the creation of high-quality collections that were both current and had significant user demand, ensuring much wider access to book material. They were also considered a promising solution to space constraints and to tackle security problems, as well as minimizing routine maintenance, such as shelving and stock management. Perhaps most problematic to these professionals was how to market electronic books to their patrons. They recognized the critical role played by the academic–student relationship and the endorsement of specific readings. Exposure to e-book content through the creation of effective discovery tools was another critical factor. Perhaps not surprisingly, librarians felt the challenge of managing budgets and of achieving value-for-money from e-books through appropriate licensing models.

Barriers to the take-up of e-books in higher and further education

Based on the work by Armstrong and Lonsdale, which identified a number of clear marketing problems for e-books, Linda Bennett of Gold Leaf (2003) undertook a further phase of market research for JISC. This sought to identify specific barriers and solutions to the uptake of e-books in UK higher and further education and addressed the views of students and academics, as well as librarians. In general, e-books were found to occupy a niche position within UK university and college libraries, based on a number of factors. One undoubted cause has been the lack of relevant content in the marketplace, a legacy from the beginnings of e-book publishing in the US. Other issues for libraries included the availability of suitable formats and of an affordable licensing model, which widens access to material. Bennett's report is very strong on her analysis of communication channels between the major stakeholders in the information chain: publishers, booksellers, academic staff, librarians and students. She is adamant that these need to be transformed. She is extremely upbeat about the future, provided some of the current obstacles can be overcome. Her research also looked at academic attitudes in universities and colleges. Here, she found a decided lack of knowledge of the medium, including a number of prejudices against the format and some doubts about the benefits, both it terms of teaching and research activity. Academics are unsure how to integrate them into their work; will the integration be at the surface level (access to content) or deeper (new ways of using books within the research and learning situation)? Academics are culturally conditioned to use the printed book, and it will take time for them to discover how to integrate e-books into their work and to exploit the medium's capabilities.

E-book forms

Research undertaken by Armstrong and Lonsdale (1998) reported a range of evidence on the monograph publishing industry and the future of the electronic monograph. Although the report raised a number of general worries about the impermanence and potential instability of the e-monograph, at the same time it highlighted the new possibilities created by the concept of the digital monograph. These included cross-referencing, embedded links to other full-text materials and powerful search tools. Watkinson's (2001) study of the monograph 'crisis' concluded that a radically new approach would be needed to address the decline. Since publication of the reports, major monograph publishers have indeed entered the marketplace with highly innovative products, not least in the humanities, where the monograph is the major channel for communication of research and for scholarly discourse, and the social sciences. Of particular note is Oxford Scholarship Online (www.oxfordscholarship.com) positioned not as an e-book but as a research and study tool. Oxford's product embraces opportunities for applying granularity to material but also extends outwards into a comprehensive web of resources. In practice, this means reference linking to other resources, the provision of keywords and abstracts at book and chapter level, the integration of object identifiers at book and chapter level, the availability of MARC21 records, SFX compliance, and so on. Scholars will benefit from being able not only to search across a large collection of books for relevant titles, but also explore deeper into segments of a specific book.

E-books supporting change in the nature of research

The nature of research is changing, becoming far more collaborative and interdisciplinary, and we need to take a more holistic view of the scholarly communication process. The e-books of the future are likely to build a community of scholarship around them, and that dialogue is likely to create a forum for a much wider audience, including practitioners and policy makers. Their shape, in terms of content and its presentation, and the communication dynamics, may well differ from one 'discipline' (or perhaps we should use terms like 'knowledge domain' or 'knowledge community') to another. As we have seen with the printed book, new technology will inevitably mould and change the form of human discourse and thought. It is even likely that the electronic text will change the structures of disciplines themselves and that they may start to evolve in new directions as a result. Attention is a likely measurement of success, and the impact on scholarship, as well as on policies and outcomes, may well be a feature of this future discourse. Books and book chapters could carry impact factors in just the same way that journals do.

Armstrong and Lonsdale (2003) wonder whether the journal and monograph will eventually merge as a form, the monograph providing a type of extended context. The narrative structure of the monograph may also change. There is again the question of whether publishers should follow the printed model when moving into electronic publishing or, as Lynch (2001) suggests, create an entirely new model for the medium. Print favours long narratives and certain types of reading, while the electronic media is predisposed towards modular, classified and indexed chunks of content. The ACLS History E-Book Project (www.historye-book.org) is a funded initiative with a vision to develop e-books that exploit technology in new ways. For forthcoming titles that are 'born digital' it has sought to encourage scholars to present material using innovative means, rethinking the relationship between narrative, data and other evidence.

Academic and professional texts

A real growth area for e-books is in textbooks, manuals, reference books and professional books, as their role and use of content lend themselves readily to the digital environment. There are already a number of excellent electronic reference works on the market, both single and multiple publisher products, providing collections of cross-searchable material, which is constantly updated with current or edited information.

Publishers have been extremely cautious about entering the market for electronic textbooks. Supplementary learning materials accompanying textbooks are now commonplace, but they are likely to evolve to become electronic learning materials in their own right. An e-textbook will become, in effect, an integral part of an e-learning system. It will link to a variety of learning objects, assessment tools and course management tools, and give the student a variety of paths through the material. Both the publisher and the institution will want to assemble and reassemble material flexibly: 'one of the major effects of the evolution of electronic distribution of information is the growing awareness that information should be packaged and repackaged to accommodate specific market needs and the new distribution technologies' (Kist, 1987).

Students want highly customized content that integrates seamlessly with other material and which directly supports a learning plan. Their need is for material that is searchable, which they can shape around their particular learning path. On a purely practical level, they want an alternative to carrying around heavy textbooks with a short 'shelf life'. The growth of online learning environments will support the increase in chunking of books. Students are likely to be early adopters of e-books, and increased support from lecturers and improved visibility of e-book content, for example, through online learning environments, will boost interest and demand. As Linda Bennett (2004) highlights, embedding e-books into institutional learning will require effective partnering between publishers, course tutors and libraries.

E-books and libraries

The 'one size fits all' model is not likely to serve the library of the future. If the e-book becomes a component of a new system of scholarly communication, then libraries will need to redefine themselves around the specific communities of users they serve. A library will not be just a place with a large collection of material but an organization that relates far more closely to its community. Such personalized systems of the future will 'learn' about the user, their preferences and information needs and will mediate between the user and a world of knowledge resources.

This makes marketing a critical issue for libraries. Librarians will need to understand how a particular scholarly community operates and interacts with other communities, the type of materials it uses and the means of access. It calls for a scholarly communication model mapped around key user groups and this mapping of needs will shape future collections strategies. The ability to understand how users discover and interact with knowledge and information is vital. The model will be dynamic, reflecting changes in current knowledge development, the increasing interdisciplinary nature and team-based approach of academic work. Libraries have traditionally dealt with fixed text. We are now moving to a world of dynamic text, with granular and personalized content. Our sense of a 'publication' will change as a consequence. Library strategists will need to reflect on these scenarios for the future. Lanham (1993) contends that the role of librarians will be to construct human attention structures, rather than assemble a collection of books according to standard rules. Metadata and object identifiers at a granular level are something that publishers certainly are recognizing as important to the chunking and integration of material into learning and research environments. Librarians too will recognize that metadata schemes can be the catalyst for using materials in new ways and for bringing user and content together.

Business models

A variety of economic models have been tried in the e-book marketplace, including ownership in perpetuity, pay-per-view, annual subscription and short-term licensing. One publisher, Taylor & Francis, offers customers a choice of all these models through its 'e-book store'. Publishers now have a unique opportunity with e-books to develop a much stronger relationship with the end user and to understand the type of material demanded by customers, its presentation and use.

For libraries, the trend towards collection access rather than collection ownership is likely to favour models other than those of actual ownership. The trend is certainly for flat-rate subscription but libraries are likely to want to make use of all the models. Much depends on the life-cycle of certain books, however; monographs in certain disciplines, where the rate of obsolescence is much slower, may lend themselves to access in perpetuity. We are aware, of course, that libraries have often managed their budgets by investing more in journal subscriptions, at the expense of books. Where library budgets are structured around book acquisition via outright purchase, then the subscription model can pose a problem when library budgets lack flexibility. Quite often, e-books are bought from separate allocations for new electronic products but, clearly, this is not a long term answer.

As we have seen, offering much wider access to books is one of the key benefits of the electronic format, and therefore simultaneous use is a critical factor for librarians. However, this can create a tension between suppliers and libraries, caused by the potential impact of multiple simultaneous access on certain revenue streams, particularly textbooks. Publishers cannot afford to lose income by negotiating institutional licences for multiple users to electronic textbooks and this must be recognized by librarians. An inclusive model needs to evolve, which gives students access to the material they need but where costs are met partly by the student, partly by the institution. New methods of payment, including micro-payment models – for example through mobile telephone accounts – are likely to encourage students to buy material direct from a publisher or intermediaries. The 'slice and dice' model gives students the opportunity to acquire only the material they need, at a price they can afford.

Major publishers and aggregators have signed significant deals with consortia for access to their e-book services. Rejecting the Big Deal model, however, institutions want to shape their e-book collections around their user communities, either by a 'pick and mix' approach to the titles offered by a publisher or aggregator, or by participating in a shared deal for a large collection of books with other libraries.

For all libraries, but particularly those on small budgets, free e-books are an important asset. Project Gutenberg is a well known example that started in 1971, growing into a library of over 4000 public domain works. The Arts & Humanities Data Service in the UK (Berglund et al., 2003) undertook a very useful survey on the availability and use of free e-books. The report provides a useful map of key sources. Their freedom from copyright restriction means that these materials can be repurposed more easily for integration into learning environments tailored around institutional need. However, institutions should also recognize that many of the collections are of variable quality in terms of text presentation and versioning. The frequent lack of structural mark-up and metadata means that time and money must often be invested in order to make works usable within a learning environment.

Conclusion: roles for the future

Print technology has evolved into a highly sophisticated model, with indexes, tables of content, pagination and other features. Publishing is a business that provides readers with high quality content, with the benefits of provenance and branding. However, the electronic world does challenge well established notions around the printed book. As we have seen, our scholarly communication system and the traditional information chain are changing. New forms of knowledge creation and communication are made possible, new kinds of knowledge structures will emerge and we will interact with content in new ways. The question is how the key stakeholders within the scholarly communication chain position themselves to maintain and enhance the knowledge flows made possible by electronic networks. Feather (2003) questions whether publishers themselves will have a role: 'the problem for publishers is to find their place in the knowledge economy'. As the electronic book becomes one building block within a system of multimedia communication, so other players may find themselves with a stake and a reason to be involved with new means of communicating and sharing knowledge:

> The printed book – so recently the iconic cultural product of western society – suddenly seems in real danger of displacement not merely as a medium of entertainment and a tool of leisure (where it has long been under threat), but also in the sphere where it has been almost unchallenged for 500 years as the container and purveyor of learning and ideas. Publishing itself is increasingly seen as merely one part of a larger complex of industries, which includes the mass media, other leisure activities and other aspects of culture.   (Feather, 2003)

At the other end of the traditional chain, electronic content is being created within academic institutions themselves. The starting point may be simple lecture slides, handouts and other electronic content, which is currently populating online learning environments. Institutional repositories are still in their infancy, but such content and communication channels will become increasingly sophisticated. Indeed, the consultants Education for Change (2003) suggest that any set of digital 'learning objects', grouped together in a clearly defined path of learning and which are properly indexed and referenced, may be called an 'e-textbook'. They contend that new entrants in the market are likely to come from non-mainstream publishers, since there will be greater willingness to take a risk.

The challenge in the short term for e-book creators and publishers is to produce content that exploits the electronic environment but which also enhances the reading or study experience for the end user. At the same time, the printed book brings with it a number of fundamental issues that must be addressed. They include version control and archiving.

Staley (2003) wonders how profound the impact of the computer on the book will be. After all, the printed book is an amazing piece of technology:

> We have to remind ourselves that if, how, and whenever we move beyond the book, that movement will not embody a movement from something natural or human to something artificial – from nature to

technology – since writing, and printing, and books are about as technological as one can get. Books, after all, are teaching and communicating *machines*.   (Landow, 1997)

What is clear is that our current view of e-books is strongly rooted in the world of print, and we still have quite a long road ahead: 'the transition from the codex to the presently evolving electronic book, the fourth form of the book in history, will not happen overnight' (Kilgour, 1998). E-books are the 'last mile' to the electronic library (O'Leary, 2001). It makes for a truly fascinating journey for all of us involved.

References

Armstrong, C. J. and Lonsdale, R. E. (1998) *The Publishing of Electronic Scholarly Monographs and Textbooks*, www.ukoln.ac.uk/dlis/models/studies/elec-pub/elec-pub.htm.

Armstrong, C. J. and Lonsdale, R. E. (2003) *The E-book Mapping Exercise*, www.jisc.ac.uk/coll_ebookstudy1.html.

Bennett, L. (2004) E-niche in Academe, *The Bookseller*, (2 January), 20–1.

Berglund, Y., Morrison, A., Wilson, R. and Wynne, M. (2003) *An Investigation into Free E-books*, www.jisc.ac.uk/coll_ebookstudy4.html.

Education for Change Ltd (2003) *A Strategy and Vision for the Future of Electronic Textbooks in UK Further and Higher Education*, www.jisc.ac.uk/coll_ebookstudy3.html.

Eisenstein, E. L. (1979) *The Printing Press as an Agent of Change in Europe: communications and cultural transformations in early-modern Europe*, 2 vols, Cambridge, Cambridge University Press.

Enzensberger, H. M. (1970) Constituents of a Theory of the Media. In Druckrey, T. (1996) *Electronic Culture: technology and visual representation*, New York, Aperture.

Feather, J. (2003) *Communicating Knowledge: publishing in the 21st century*, Munich, KG Saur.

Gold Leaf (2003) *Promoting the Uptake of E-books in Higher and Further Education*, www.jisc.ac.uk/coll_ebookstudy2.html.

Johns, A. (1998) *The Nature of the Book: print and knowledge in the making*, Chicago, University of Chicago Press.

Kilgour, F. G. (1998) *The Evolution of the Book*, Oxford, Oxford University Press.

Kist, J. (1987) *Electronic Publishing: looking for a blueprint*, London, Croom Helm.

Landow, G. P. (1997) *Hypertext 2.0.*, rev. edn, Baltimore, Johns Hopkins University Press.

Lanham, R. A. (1993) *The Electronic Word: democracy, technology and the arts*, Chicago, University of Chicago Press.

Lynch, C. (1999) Electrifying the Book, *Library Journal NetConnect* supplement, (15 October), 3–6.

Lynch, C. (2001) The Battle to Define the Future of the Book in the Digital World, *First Monday*, **6** (6), www.firstmonday.dk/issues/issue6_6/lynch.

O'Leary, M. (2001) E-book Scenarios Updated, *Online*, **27** (5), http://infotoday.com/online/sep03/oleary.shtml.

Olson, D. R. (1994) *The World on Paper: the conceptual and cognitive implications of writing and reading*, Cambridge, Cambridge University Press.

Staley, D. J. (2003) The Future of the Book in a Digital Age, *Futurist*, (September–October), 18–22.

Watkinson, A. (2001) *Electronic Solutions to the Problems of Monograph Publishing*, Resource: The Council for Museums, Archives and Libraries, http://mla.gov.uk/information/research/respubs2001.asp.

9

Economics of publishing and the future of scholarly communication

John Houghton

Introduction

This chapter reviews and synthesizes recent analysis of the economics of scientific and professional publishing. It suggests that the underlying economic characteristics of information in print and online forms go a long way towards explaining the recent evolution of the scholarly communication system, the emergence of the so called crisis in scholarly communication and such recent developments as the Big Deal subscription model for access to online journals. The chapter argues that digitization and online access and distribution fundamentally change the underlying economic characteristics of content products, and that these changes will affect existing business models, cost and industry structures. At the same time, research practices are changing, bringing new communication and dissemination needs. Together, these forces are changing scholarly communication and scientific publishing in ways that are yet to become entirely clear. The chapter concludes that, whatever the future holds, any new system must take account of the roles of existing stakeholders, objects and activities; the emerging needs of researchers; the emerging opportunities afforded by rapidly developing information and communication technologies and applications; and the underlying economic characteristics of information in its various forms.

A crisis in scholarly communication

Exploring the economics of the creation, production and distribution of scholarly and scientific content in the print era reveals a good deal about the impact of the incentive structure on authors, and how it combined with the economic characteristics of information to shape a crisis in scholarly communication (Houghton, 2001). Many commentators have pointed to the rapid increase in prices for scholarly and scientific content, especially journals in the science, technology and medical fields (Cummings, et al., 1992; Bosch, 1999; King and Tenopir, 1999; Houghton, 2001; and so on). Price increases have been substantially above the underlying rate of inflation, and they have now spread into other areas (e.g. business and management) and to monograph pricing (Watkins, 2001; La Manna, 2003; Steele, 2003; Bergstrom and Bergstrom, 2004). By the late 1990s, it seemed that the system was becoming unsustainable. Harnad (2001) concluded that commercial publishers' price levels made most articles in the commercial literature inaccessible to most potential users.

Van Orsdel and Born (2003) looked at the prices charged for those journals appearing in ISI citation indexes over the period 1999 to 2003. They found that the average price of titles originating in North America increased by 41% and the average price of those originating in Europe increased by 33%. Prices for US originating titles in the *Science Citation Index* increased by 40% and those for non-US titles increased by 30%, compared with increases of 40% and 38% for titles from the *Arts and Humanities Citation Index*, and 44% and 36% for titles in the *Social Sciences Citation Index*, respectively. As Figure 9.1 shows, according to Blackwell's Periodical Prices Indexes, the average price of journal titles in science and technology increased by 178% over the decade from 1990 to 2000, compared with average increases of 184% for titles in medicine and 186% for titles in humanities and social sciences (SQW, 2003). At 155%, price increases over the decade for titles in the United States and Canada were lower than they were in Great Britain (204%) and elsewhere (220%).

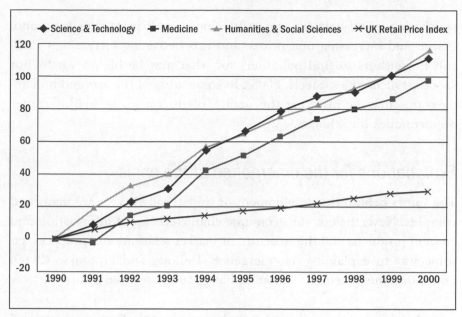

Figure 9.1   Journal price increases, 1990–2000 (indexed 1990 = 0)
(Blackwell's Periodical Prices, cited by DTI, 2002)

The US Association of Research Libraries (2003) reported that between 1986 and 2002 average serial title costs for member libraries increased by 227%, compared with a US CPI increase of 64%. Between 1986 and 2000, median serial titles purchased by US research libraries decreased by 6% and monograph purchases declined 16%, and yet serials expenditure increased by 292% and monograph expenditure increased by 48%. Similar data from the Council of Australian University Librarians (2003) shows that the total number of serials titles purchased by Australian research libraries declined by almost 37% between 1986 and 1998, but total serials expenditures increased by 263% and aggregate serial unit costs increased by no less than 474%. In recent years, electronic aggregations have brought a marked reduction in serial unit costs, but research library serial expenditures continue to increase.

Not only have increasing journal prices put pressure on library budgets, but cancellations and reduced purchasing leads to reduced access. Moreover, libraries have shifted monograph budgets to serials acquisition to cover serials price increases, such that access to the monograph literature has also been affected. As a result of this decline in library

purchasing, publishers are now producing shorter print runs for monographs and increasing unit prices, and it is becoming increasingly difficult for authors to find publishers for what may be highly worthy but
specialist niche titles (Steele, 2003). In some areas of the arts and humanities, this may be affecting the nature of discourse, as well as career
opportunities for scholars.

Explanations for the emergence of the crisis

The forces behind the development of this so called crisis are many and
complex. Nevertheless, the economic characteristics of information and
content products, and the structure of market relations and practices, go
some way to explaining its emergence. DeLong and Froomkin (2000)
noted that the system of market exchange rests on three pillars:

- excludability – the ability to exclude some people from property and
  thereby create the basis for exchange
- rivalry – that the consumption of something by one person prevents
  others from consuming it too
- transparency – the ability of consumers to see what they need, what is
  for sale and be able to judge its value to them relative to other things.

Excludability

Excludability depends upon property rights and the rule of law; transparency underpins the functioning of markets as systems of exchange
and rivalry characterizes most goods and services. For example, when
buying a pair of shoes one can inspect them and try them on, decide how
much one is willing to pay and shop around until one finds a
quality–price trade-off one is happy with, and once one buys and is wearing one's shoes no one else can be wearing them too. Moreover, the cost
of producing another pair for someone else is more or less the same as
the cost of producing the first pair – depending on whether the producer is facing increasing or decreasing returns to scale at the current
level of production.

Rivalry

The key to understanding publishing is to realize that information is not like shoes. Information is, basically, non-rivalrous in consumption. If one person consumes a cheese sandwich, it is gone; no one else can consume it too. If, however, one person reads a journal article and gains knowledge from it, the information in the article remains. Any number of people can consume it again. This 'scarcity-defying expansiveness of knowledge' is one of its most important defining features (Stiglitz, 1999). It means that ideas and information exhibit very different economic characteristics from the goods and services of the industrial economy, and that the social value of ideas and information increases to the degree they can be shared with and used by others. The more such information goods are consumed, the greater the social return on investment in them.

Transparency

Information is also an experience good. Until one has bought and consumed the information one does not know its value, and once one has it is too late to decide not to buy it. So, the decision to buy is not made on the basis of the content, directly, but on the basis of other cues. For example, a researcher new to a field might make extensive use of abstract and keyword searching to identify articles to read. More experienced researchers might use other signals, such as who the authors are, the institutional affiliation of the authors, knowledge of the work of the editor and editorial board members, or of the title of the journal. Because the decision to consume is made in these ways, these things become important sources of value for publishers. Content may be king, but authorship, quality control and branding are important determinants of its price.

Costs and pricing of books and journals

Books and journals are typical information products in that first copy costs are high while the marginal costs of (re)production are low. This has a profound effect on costs and pricing, with circulation a major determinant of costs. Some analysts have suggested that the increase in the number of new journal titles has lowered the average circulation of journals and thereby increased fixed costs (first copy costs) as a share of total costs (Noll and Steinmueller, 1992; King and Tenopir, 1999; King and Tenopir, 2000; and so on.). King and Tenopir (2000) analysed journal production costs between 1975 and 1995 (in the print era). Their modelling showed a decline of around 20% in the average cost per page published, but they found that the increase in the number of journal titles, the number of articles per issue and the number of pages per article contributed to increasing costs overall. As journal prices increased and subscriptions were cancelled, average costs increased, further increasing prices and encouraging more cancellations – leading to a vicious circle of journal price increases, to which limited substitutability and low price elasticity of demand have also contributed.

Particular journal titles create monopolies, in that they cannot be substituted easily with alternative titles. There are many factors at play, including high levels of branding and the long term influence of titles through citation patterns and impact factors. Institutional incentives exacerbate the problem, with promotion, tenure and funding allocations in universities and research institutions often linked to publication in a few key refereed journals. Research library purchasing practices have also contributed to the problem. Journal titles and books typically competed with each other as substitutes across broad fields of research and scholarship, rather than being considered separately; the budget for purchasing in each field has typically been determined by the strategic priorities of the institution, such that titles across fields do not compete on cost per use; the budget for each field has been determined largely independently of price information, and largely independently of demand or usage; and budget allocations to each field have taken little or no account of cost per use across fields (McCabe, 1998a, 1998b, 1998c; Houghton, 2001). These features of the print publication acquisition system led to a failure of market signals (especially of price signals to the end users) and very low price elasticity of demand, with large price changes having relatively little effect on demand.

It has also been suggested that some of the larger commercial publishers exercise monopoly power (Hunter, 1998; Odlyzko, 1998; Wyly, 1998; McCabe, 1998a, 1998b, 1998c, 1999, 2002). Evidence marshalled in support of these assertions has included the relative prices for content from commercial and non-profit publishers, publisher operating margins and profits. Kean (2003) pointed to a difference in the rate of price increases for journals from non-profit US society and commercial publishers, with prices for society journals increasing by an average of 7.5% per annum between 1988 and 2003, compared with 9.5% per annum for all US periodicals. Similarly, Bergstrom and Bergstrom (2004) have shown that journal costs per page and per citation are substantially higher for commercial publishers than non-profit publishers. Wyly (1998) noted that, in 1997, Reed Elsevier enjoyed a higher net profit margin than 473 of the S&P 500 listed companies; Wolters Kluwer provided higher return on equity than 482 of the S&P 500; and margins generated in the science, technical and medical publishing areas of these companies tend to be even higher than aggregate margins.

McCabe (1999, 2002) pioneered a portfolio approach, linking the monopoly power of the journal title as a product for which there are no close substitutes with the market power of major commercial publishers. McCabe found that prices were positively related to journal portfolio size, and that in the specific case of the merger of Wolters Kluwer and Waverly his model predicted an average price rise of between 20% and 30%. McCabe (1998b, 1998c) was also able to show that past mergers were associated with higher prices, suggesting that the Elsevier–Pergamon deal resulted in average journal price increases of 22% for former Pergamon titles and 8% for Elsevier titles. After controlling for scale economies, there remained an unexplained inflation residual that McCabe (1999) attributed to the monopoly power of the large commercial publishers.

Digitization and going online

The digitization of content and online distribution and access accentuate and sometimes change the economic characteristics of information. DeLong and Froomkin (2000) noted that digitization creates new challenges for enforcing *excludability*. Not only is it much easier and cheaper to copy and distribute digitized information in an online world, but also there is little or no degradation in the copies – with each copy being a perfect digital replica of the original. *Rivalry* is also reduced. With a print journal, only one person can be reading that copy of the journal at any given time, but in digital form any number can access and read the copy simultaneously. Thus, digitized and online content is, potentially, more nearly perfectly non-rivalrous in consumption. *Transparency* in the digital world is more problematic. Because information is an experience good (the consumers do not know what it is worth until they have consumed it) the availability of information about information is a key element in valuation. The internet has introduced new and more accessible sources of information about information and about its pricing. It is now possible to do far more detailed research about the qualities and prices of an intended purchase (DeLong and Froomkin, 2000). Nevertheless, the inherent lack of transparency of information goods remains.

Digitization and online access and distribution also change cost structures. Characteristically, digitized products have high first copy costs and very low subsequent copy or marginal costs. Online distribution tends to reduce marginal costs of production to near zero. When content is packaged on compact disc, shrink wrapped with installation and operating instructions and distributed through a wholesale-retail distribution channel there remain significant costs in the production and distribution of copies. By contrast, making the same content and instructions available online reduces these producers' costs dramatically, with no physical (re)production and distribution activities and no inventory. There may be some increase in the producers' technical infrastructure costs, but the impact of online distribution tends to be to increase first copy costs, reduce marginal cost of production to near zero and shift distribution costs to the consumer (externalizing the costs).

Online publisher business models

Current and emerging content business models can be seen as responses to the changed economic characteristics of content brought about by digitization and online distribution and access. They emerge as publishers seek ways to re-create the conditions of excludability and rivalry. Offline conditions of rivalry have been re-created by publishers through the introduction of user licences that specify such conditions of access as the allowed number of concurrent users. These are often supported by technical means, such as IP authentication, software controlling simultaneous access and so forth. Transparency is more problematic. The functioning of markets requires complete transparency, but profit maximization may not. Striking the best balance between transparency and exclusion is a key element of publisher business models.

Generally, digitization and online access facilitate transparency, making it easier for consumers to find information about information and experience samples, and easier for producers to produce indexes, abstracts, summaries and samples of their content along with information as to its popularity (number of hits, downloads, citations, and so on) and its use (for example 'readers who downloaded x also downloaded y'). However, as DeLong and Froomkin (2000) pointed out, there can be both anti-competitive and genuine reasons for producers to seek to limit transparency (especially in relation to price) and for consumers to seek to limit transparency (especially in relation to the use of information about their personal downloading activities). For example, a supplier that enhances its service with additional information for would-be consumers will be unable to compete with suppliers that do not bear the cost of doing so, if consumers can access the information and benefit from it, but then use an intelligent agent or 'shop bot' to find the lowest price and purchase from the lower cost supplier (DeLong and Froomkin, 2000).

One of the ways in which publishers have responded to both the opportunity and threat of digitization and online distribution and access is to move from supplying a good to supplying a service. For publishers of computer software this has meant versioning, providing access to ongoing fixes and upgrades, the use of licences locking customers into fixes and upgrades as a condition of support and moving towards an application services provider model based on pay-per-use. Similarly, scientific and professional publishers have attempted to shift revenue from accession to subscription (for instance from monographs to serials). Providing access on subscription changes the one-off sale of an information good into the ongoing services of access to information. It also acts to lock consumers into ongoing payments and guarantees a revenue stream for the publisher.

Bakos and Brynjolfsson (2000) explored the impacts of digitization and online distribution on aggregation and disaggregation (bundling and unbundling). They suggested that lower distribution costs tend to make unbundling more attractive for sellers, while lower marginal costs of production tend to favour bundling. Operating the infrastructure and mechanisms for pay-per-view and associated payments represent unavoidable costs in the unbundling model, whereas near zero marginal cost favours bundling – the more so where advertising and marketing costs can be significantly reduced by aggregating consumers. Bundling has technical and economic drivers, and the internet has radically changed the techno-economics of distribution and opened up new possibilities for profit maximization. Goods that were previously aggregated to save transaction or distribution costs may be disaggregated (for example newspapers), but new aggregations may emerge to exploit the potential of bundling for profit maximization (Bakos and Brynjolfsson, 2000, 117).

Varian (1995) provided an outline of how bundling works in scientific and professional publishing, in which he noted that bundling is profitable because it reduces the heterogeneity of the consumers' willingness to pay. If different consumers have a different willingness to pay and the producer cannot price discriminate, all the consumers buy the product at the price of the buyer with the lowest willingness to pay. By creating the bundle, the producer can sell at the *average* willingness to pay, which is typically more profitable. Some analysts have extended the logic of bundling from the content itself to subscription (bundling over time) and site licensing (bundling users) (Bakos and Brynjolfsson, 1999; Bakos, Brynjolfsson and Lichtman, 1999; Bakos and Brynjolfsson, 2000). Just as different consumers may have a different willingness to pay, so too the same consumer may have a different willingness to pay at different times. If provision of access over time costs very little, it may be more profitable to provide a long term subscription than for individual uses in short periods of time (Bakos and Brynjolfsson, 2000, 131). Similarly, site licensing aggregates individual subscribers and allows the supplier to charge at the individuals' average willingness to pay. Site licensing may also reduce marketing and distribution costs, thereby contributing to greater efficiency. However, as a sale to an institution rather than an individual final consumer, price elasticity of demand is likely to be lower.

The Big Deal

Current practice in scientific and professional publishing combines these things into the Big Deal, in which publishers aggregate their journal titles and provide access for multiple users through site licences on subscription. There are many potentially positive consequences, through reduced costs and enhanced access. For example, it is evident that research library serial unit (title) costs have fallen. Nevertheless, the Big Deal may also exacerbate the journals crisis. In a world of individual subscriptions to print journals, only those journal titles that can maintain sufficient circulation to cover costs can survive. As circulation falls, first copy costs account for a greater share of total costs and average unit costs increase. If priced at or near average cost, prices increase and subscriptions fall further, and so on until the journal is withdrawn from the market. In the world of the Big Deal, however, it is in the interest of the publisher to offer as large a bundle (as many titles) as possible. As long as the bundle can be priced accordingly there is no pressure to axe individual journal titles. Low demand content may remain on the market longer than it otherwise would, and the fixed costs of low use and low citation titles remain in the system. So, while from the publishers' point of view bundling, site licensing and selling on subscription make sense, it may not make sense for the system as a whole.

Changing research practices and emerging needs

Scientific and professional publishing is part of the wider innovation system. That system and roles within it are changing. Importantly for scholarly communication, there are some quite fundamental changes in the practice of research and in the ways in which knowledge is produced that have implications for its communication and dissemination.

A new mode of knowledge production has emerged over recent years, which is often characterized in terms of the differences between it (Mode 2) and traditional, disciplinary research (Mode 1) (Gibbons et al., 1994). With the emergence of this new mode of research there is increasing diversity in the location of research activities; an increasing focus on interdisciplinary, multidisciplinary and transdisciplinary research; an increasing focus on problems, rather than techniques; greater emphasis on collaborative work and communication; and greater emphasis on more diverse and informal modes of communication. Most analysts see Mode 1 and Mode 2 research operating in parallel, with the new mode of knowledge production supplementing rather than replacing traditional 'science' (Gibbons, 2001; McWilliam et al., 2002). While there has been lively debate about the conceptualization of the emergence of a new mode of knowledge production (Nowotny, Scott and Gibbons, 2001, 2003), one can find evidence of the characteristic changes in research practices suggested by it (Houghton, Steele and Henty, 2003; and so on).

There are fundamental information and communication differences between the traditional and emerging modes of knowledge production. Whereas traditional disciplinary research has formalized systems for scholarly communication, peer review and quality control, education, training and accreditation, the new mode tends to rely more on informal communication and dissemination – with the emergence of Mode 2 research facilitated by the availability of improved means of communication and the widespread diffusion of information and communication technologies (Meyer-Krahmer, 1997, 309). Mainstream scientific and professional publishing has evolved over many years, during which traditional disciplinary research has been the dominant mode of knowledge production. As a result, the existing mainstream system is better suited to the traditional than it is to the new mode of knowledge production (Mackenzie Owen, 2002; Houghton, Steele and Henty, 2003). Consequently, not only is there a crisis in the traditional system of journal publishing, but the system may also be failing to provide adequate and appropriate support for emerging modes of research.

Emerging opportunities and future directions
The open access/open source movement

The rapid development of information and communication technologies and applications is opening up new opportunities. Perhaps the most fundamental challenge for publishing arises from the open access/open source (OA/OS) movement. OA/OS has emerged in recent years as an alternative, and appears to be gaining momentum and credibility (Suber,

2004). OA/OS challenges the assumptions of the traditional market model. Instead of contriving ways to (re)create excludability and rivalry for information goods, OA/OS champions the public good view of information (Berry, 2000).

Approaching the two core questions for public goods, the motivation to produce in the first place and the problem of free-riders, Weber (2001) argued that the problem of free-riders does not arise where something is non-rivalrous *and* there are positive network externalities. Where one person's consumption of something has no impact on the potential of others to consume, free-riders may be tolerated. Where there are benefits to all individual users from the expansion of use the contribution of all users, including free-riders, is positive. An example might be the advantage to an individual user of a software package from the expansion of the number of other people using compatible file formats, thereby making communication and file exchange easier, regardless of whether those users are using legal or pirated copies of the software. This combination of non-rivalrous consumption and positive network effects characterizes anti-rival goods (Weber, 2001).

As Weber (2001) noted, a number of arguments have been put forward to explain individual motivation to participate in the collective production of open source software. These include credentialism, with the rewards of providing an elegant solution to a problem reaped in terms of enhanced reputation among a peer group and the signalling of capabilities to potential future employers (Lerner and Tirole, 2000); and abundance and the emergence of a culture of gift giving, with social status dependent upon what one gives away rather than what one owns (Kuwabara, 2000). There are many parallels between open source and open access in scientific and professional publishing. The motivation for collective production of research-based scientific and scholarly publications rests on both economic and social foundations. Recognition and reputation among a peer group are important, and research careers are built on the production of research outputs and publication. Moreover, funding for future work is often tied to publication. Hence, there has been government-supported collective production through public support for research, and the researchers' desire to publish explains their preparedness to give the content away in exchange for its publication and distribution. Online publications are non-rival in the sense that they are not exhausted in consumption. Moreover, from the collective point of view, there are clear benefits to the widest possible dissemination of new scientific and technical knowledge (positive network externalities), while from the point of view of individual researchers and authors, increased circulation and citation are positive. To that extent, scientific and scholarly publications can be said to be 'anti-rival'. Hence, there exist conditions for successful collective production, but how might distribution be re-engineered to support it?

The expanding role of knowledge in the economy, increased attention to the role of knowledge in such areas as the management of health and the environment, changing research practices and new access and communication needs will all play a role in the future evolution of scientific and professional publishing. To date, most attention has been directed to re-engineering journal publishing, with the focus on developing sustainable pricing models that cover unavoidable costs (for instance peer review). Current pricing practices include various mixes of five basic models:

- subscriptions – where individual and institutional subscribers pay for access to single or bundled titles
- pay-per-use – where individual or institutional users pay for access to single articles
- advertiser supported distribution – where advertisers seeking to sell to readers contribute to cover some or all of the costs of production and distribution
- author charges – where authors contribute some or all of the costs of publication
- institutionally supported open archives – where institutions provide digital repositories for their communities.

Open access publishing supported by author charges

One recent development to have gained considerable momentum has been open access publishing supported by author charges (SQW, 2003: 27). There is a distinction here between open access publishing, which involves open and free access to published content combined with author charges, and open access archives or repositories, which involve open and free access to a range of material held and maintained by organizations (such as universities) on behalf of their communities. However, it is not clear that it is a sustainable way forward (Willinsky, 2003; Zandonella, 2003; McCabe and Snyder, 2004). There are potential difficulties in moving to any system that introduces means (rather than merit) as a condition of publishing. Where publication is supported through research grant funding there may be further accentuation of the Matthew Principle (after the Bible passage: 'For unto every one that hath shall be given, and he shall have abundance: but from him that hath not shall be taken away even that which he hath', Matthew 25:29, now commonly paraphrased as 'the rich get richer and the poor get poorer') with publication dependent on research funding and research funding dependent on publication. Moreover, author-supported models may introduce an incentive to publish less at the individual, institutional and perhaps even national levels, which is the antithesis of what most proponents of the public good argument and open access seek to achieve. Conversely, where author charges are levied for accepted articles, there is an economic incentive for publishers to accept a higher proportion of articles for publication, which has negative implications for quality and scholarship.

Perhaps more importantly, moving from a user pays system to what is in effect a producer pays system raises both equity issues and questions of practicality. In fields where there is extensive application of research, such as medicine, engineering, computer science, management, and so on, many of the users (readers) do not contribute as authors. BioMed Central is one example, where university-based researchers pay to be published while their readers, many of whom are in the private sector, access the work free of charge and apply its findings in their business and professional practices. Such a system may reflect the public good nature of knowledge, but leaves unanswered the question of how its collective production is to be funded equitably. With open access publication and author charges, many major research institutions could well pay more to support publishing than they have for journal subscriptions. In its submission to the UK House of Commons Science and Technology Committee Inquiry into Scientific Publications, for example, Elsevier (2004) suggested that:

while Britain's spending on journal subscriptions currently amounts to 3.3% of the world's total, UK researchers contribute a much higher 5% of all articles published globally. As a result, we estimate that the UK Government, foundations, universities and researchers could together pay 30–50% more for STM journals in an Open Access [publishing] system than they do today.   (Elsevier, 2004, 2).

Any advantage such a system might bring in terms of access to the journal literature for researchers in the poorer countries as readers, must be set against their increased exclusion as authors.

As the systems of scholarly and scientific communication evolve in the digital online era one would expect there to be changes in what is valued and where value lies. Open access (without author charges) has the potential to add value for researchers as readers and authors by extending dissemination through standardized harvestable systems and reducing the time delay in publication through a system of pre- and post-print posting. One potentially important contribution of institutionally based open access repositories or archives may be their greater accommodation of emerging modes of research, by enabling non- or trans-disciplinary modes of research dissemination associated with organizations, such as research centres or universities, rather than a discipline. Lynch suggested that the development of institutional repositories was:

a new strategy that allows universities to apply serious, systematic leverage to accelerate changes taking place in scholarship and scholarly communication . . . scaling up beyond ad-hoc alliances, partnerships, and support arrangements with a few select faculty pioneers exploring more transformative new uses of the digital medium.   (Lynch, 2003).

Roles of key stakeholders, objects and activities

Crow (2002) suggested that institutional repositories centralize, preserve and make accessible an institution's intellectual capital and form part of a global system of decentralized, distributed repositories. This appeal to institutions highlights one of the keys to achieving a sustainable re-engineering of the system of scientific publishing and scholarly communication – namely, that proposed changes must take account of the roles of key stakeholders, objects and activities as it (re)combines new research practices and needs with emerging ICT-enabled opportunities and the historical structures and mechanisms of publishing. The following short examples demonstrate some emerging possibilities.

When looking at key objects the principal questions are: what role does the object play and are there viable alternatives? Perhaps the most central object is the journal. For authors the journal title is a brand, built on quality control, prestige of editorial affiliations, citation and impact factors. For readers, however, the availability of online journal databases and tendency to search online by author or keyword mean that readers are increasingly accessing articles independently of journal titles, and the journal is becoming somewhat less important to readers. The journal has also played other, 'non-publishing' roles for the research community. For example, journals have formed the basis for networks of scholars, for which the editor forms a focal point around which members of the editorial board, regular reviewers, contributors and readers orbit. Such networks of scholarship can be extremely important (Houghton, 2001; Houghton, Steele and Henty, 2003). Journals have also provided fora for ongoing discussion of particular topics of interest to the scholarly communities they serve (SQW, 2003). However, for all of these there are increasingly viable alternatives based on emerging information and communication technologies and applications, such as discussion groups, web logs, and so on. Friedlander and Bessette (2003, 9) observed that the nature and role of scholarly journals are changing and Smith (2000) suggested that, with the development of the web, journals no longer form the primary communication medium. Indeed, for most of the roles traditionally played by the journal, alternatives are emerging.

When looking at key activities few are more central than peer review, but here too there are changes that may reduce dependence upon it. There is some concern that peer review is not working well, especially for multi-disciplinary or trans-disciplinary research (Odlyzko, 2002; Rowland, 2002; Jefferson et al., 2003; Peek, 2003). More importantly, in the increasingly multi-disciplinary, multi-site, collaborative world of research both the value of and necessity for peer review may be declining. Whereas in the past an individual scholar might report findings, it is now increasingly the case that research reports reflect the collaborative work of a number of scholars, institutions and stakeholder interests, and, by implication at least, they have all seen, vetted and, effectively, peer reviewed the material. Again there are new, technology-based alternatives emerging, such as online commentary, threaded discussion (Nadasdy, 1997; Varian, 1998; Singer, 2000) and procedures for and controls over posting to archives and repositories – such as institutional affiliation and status, or what Kling, Spector and McKim (2002) referred to as Guild Publishing and the substitution of peer review by career review.

This is not to suggest the immediate abandonment of particular objects or activities, but rather that their roles may be changing and the evolution of the system may involve the dissolution of existing and emergence of new combinations of objects, activities and responsibilities – such as, for example, the decline of commercial publisher control over peer-reviewed journal titles and the rise of institutional open access repositories and archives populated by free-standing digital objects of all kinds, with quality control based around career review and online user commentary, and impacts measured as hits, downloads, citations and links. Such a reconfiguration of objects and activities would probably provoke adjustment of stakeholder responsibilities (Mackenzie Owen, 2002) – such as, for example, large commercial publishing firms shifting their emphasis from content control to value-adding activities built around open access objects (for example harvesting content from open access repositories, packaging and adding value through the addition of archiving, abstracting and indexing and a range of powerful searching, linking and interrogation access and usage reporting functions). In the meantime, a continuation of adjustments and multiple overlapping experimental and evolutionary developments is inevitable.

Conclusion

Whatever the future holds, any new system must take account of the roles of existing stakeholders, objects and activities; the emerging needs of researchers; the emerging opportunities afforded by rapidly developing information and communication technologies and applications; and the underlying economic characteristics of information in its various forms. Only by doing so will the development of sustainable alternatives and plausible migration paths be possible.

References

Association of Research Libraries (2003) *ARL Statistics 2001–02*, www.arl.org/stats/arlstat/graphs/2002/2002t2.html [accessed March 2004].

Bakos, Y. and Brynjolfsson, E. (1999) Bundling Information Goods: pricing, profits and efficiency, *Management Science*, **45** (12), 1613–30.

Bakos, Y., Brynjolfsson, E. and Lichtman, D. G. (1999) Shared Information Goods, *Journal of Law and Economics*, **42** (4), 117–55.

Bakos, Y. and Brynjolfsson, E. (2000) Aggregation and Disaggregation of Information Goods: implications of bundling, site licensing, and micro payment systems. In Kahin, B. and Varian, H. R. (eds) *Internet Publishing and Beyond: the economics of digital information and intellectual property*, Cambridge MA, MIT Press, 114–37.

Bergstrom C. T. and Bergstrom, T. C. (2004) The Costs and Benefits of Library Site Licenses to Academic Journals, *Proceedings of the National Academy of Sciences*, **101** (3), 897–902.

Berry, R. S. (2000) Full and Open Access to Scientific Information: an academic's view, *Learned Publishing* **13** (1), 37–42, www.ingentaselect.com/alpsp/09531513/v13n1/contp1-1.htm [accessed March 2004].

Bosch, S. (1999) *The Bowker Annual Library and Book Trade Almanac*, 44th edn, New Providence NJ, R. R. Bowker, 508–9.

Council of Australian University Librarians (2003) *CAUL Statistics*, www.caul.edu.au/stats/ [accessed March 2004].

Crow, R. (2002) *The Case for Institutional Repositories: a SPARC position paper*, Scholarly Publishing and Academic Resources Coalition, www.arl.org/sparc/IR/ir.html [accessed June 2003].

Cummings, A. M., Witte, M. L, Bowen, W. G., Lazarus, L. O. and Ekman, R. H. (1992) *University Libraries and Scholarly Communication*: a study prepared for the Andrew W. Mellon Foundation, www.arl.org [accessed March 2004].

DeLong, J. B. and Froomkin, A. M. (2000) Speculative Microeconomics for

Tomorrow's Economy. In Kahin, B. and Varian, H. R. (eds) *Internet Publishing and Beyond: the economics of digital information and intellectual property*, Cambridge MA, MIT Press, 6–44.

Department of Trade and Industry (2002) *Publishing in the Knowledge Economy: competitiveness analysis of the UK publishing media sector*, www.dti.gov.uk/ [accessed March 2004].

Elsevier (2004) *Responses to Questions Posed by The Science and Technology Committee*, Submission to The House of Commons Science and Technology Committee Inquiry into Scientific Publications, www.biomedcentral.com/openaccess/inquiry/ [accessed March 2004].

Friedlander, A. and Bessette, R. S. (2003) *The Implications of Information Technology for Scientific Journal Publishing: a literature review*, NSF 03-323, National Science Foundation, www.nsf.gov/sbe/srs/nsf03323/ [accessed April 2004].

Gibbons, M. (2001) *Innovation and the Developing System of Knowledge Production*, paper presented at Centre for Policy Research on Science and Technology at Simon Fraser University Summer Institute on Innovation, Competitiveness and Sustainability in the North American Region, http://edie.cprost.sfu.ca/summer/papers/Michael.Gibbons.html [accessed November 2002].

Gibbons, M., Limoges, C. Nowotny, H., Schwartzman, S., Scott, P. and Trow, M. (1994) *The New Production of Knowledge: the dynamics of science and research in contemporary societies*, London, Sage.

Harnad, S. (2001) Minotaur: six proposals for freeing the refereed literature online: a comparison, *Ariadne*, **28**, www.ariadne.ac.uk/issue28/minotaur/ [accessed September 2002].

Houghton, J. W. (2001) Crisis and Transition: the economics of scholarly communication, *Learned Publishing* **14** (3), 167–76. www.catchword.com/alpsp/09531513/v14n3/contp1-1.htm [accessed March 2004].

Houghton, J. W., Steele, C. and Henty, M. (2003) *Changing Research Practices in the Digital Information and Communication Environment*, Department of Education, Science and Training, www.dest.gov.au/highered/respubs/changing_res_prac/exec_summary.htm [accessed March 2004].

Hunter, K. (1998) Electronic Journal Publishing: observations from the inside,

D-Lib, July/August, www.dlib.org/dlib/July98/ [accessed March 2004].

Jefferson, T. O. Alderson, P., Davidoff, F. and Wager, E. (2003) Editorial Peer Review for Improving the Quality of Reports of Biomedical Studies, *The Cochrane Library* 4.

Kean, G. (2003) 16th Annual Study of Journal Prices for Scientific and Medical Society Journals, *Journal Publishing* (1), www.allenpress.com/newsletters/pdf/JP-2003-01.pdf [accessed March 2004].

King, D. W. and Tenopir, C. (1999) Evolving Journal Costs: implications for publishers, libraries and readers, *Learned Publishing*, **12** (4), 251–8, www.ingentaselect.com/vl=5028935/cl=15/tt=885/ini=alpsp/nw=1/fm=docpdf/rpsv/cw/alpsp/09531513/v12n4/s3/p251 [accessed March 2004].

King, D. W. and Tenopir, C. (2000) Scholarly Journal and Digital Database Pricing; threat or opportunity?, Paper presented at *PEAK 2000*, www.si.umich.edu/PEAK-2000/king.pdf [accessed March 2004].

Kling, R., Spector, L. and McKim, G. (2002) Locally Controlled Scholarly Publishing via the Internet: the Guild model, *Journal of Electronic Publishing*, **8** (1), www.press.umich.edu/jep/08-01/kling.html [accessed August 2003].

Kuwabara, K. (2000) Linux: a bazaar at the edge of chaos, *First Monday*, **5** (3), www.firstmonday.dk/issues/issue5_3/kuwabara/ [accessed March 2004].

La Manna, M. (2003) The Economics of Publishing and the Publishing of Economics, *Library Review*, **54** (1), 18–28.

Lerner, J. and Tirole, J. (2000) *The Simple Economics of Open Source*, Working Paper 7600, National Bureau of Economic Research, http://papers.nber.org/papers/w7600 [accessed March 2004].

Lynch, C. A. (2003) Institutional Repositories: essential infrastructure for scholarship in the digital age, *ARL*, (226), 1–7, www.arl.org/newsltr/226/ir.html [accessed May 2003].

Mackenzie Owen, J. (2002) The New Dissemination of Knowledge: digital libraries and institutional roles in scholarly publishing, *Journal of Economic Methodology*, **9** (3), 275–88. See also http://citeseer.ist.psu.edu/444136.html [accessed April 2004].

McCabe, M. J. (1998a) *The Impact of Publisher Mergers on Journal Prices: a preliminary report*, Georgia Institute of Technology.

McCabe, M. J. (1998b) The Impact of Publisher Mergers on Journal Prices: a preliminary report, *ARL* (200), 3–7, www.arl.org/newsltr/200/mccabe.html [accessed August 2001].

McCabe, M. J. (1998c) The Impact of Publisher Mergers on Journal Prices: an update, *ARL* (207), www.arl.org/newsltr/207/jrnlprices.html [accessed June 2004].

McCabe, M. J. (1999) *Academic Journal Pricing and Market Power: a portfolio approach*, Georgia Institute of Technology.

McCabe, M. J. (2002) Journal Pricing and Mergers: a portfolio approach, *American Economic Review*, **92** (1), 259–69.

McCabe, M. J. and Snyder, C. M. (2004) The Economics of Open-Access Journals, Preliminary Draft, http://gsbwww.uchicago.edu/research/workshops/wto/PDF/oa03.pdf [accessed April 2004].

McWilliam, E., Taylor, P. G., Thomson, P., Green, B., Maxwell, T., Wildy, H. and Simons, D. (2002) *Research Training in Doctoral Programs: what can be learned from professional doctorates?* EIP Report 02/08, Canberra, Department of Education, Science and Training.

Meyer-Krahmer, F. (1997) Science-based Technologies and Interdisciplinary: challenges for firms and policy. In Edquist, C. (ed.) *Systems of Innovation: technologies, institutions and organizations*, London, Pinter, 298–317.

Nadasdy, Z. (1997) Electronic Journal of Cognitive and Brain Sciences: a truly all-electronic journal: let democracy replace peer review, *Journal of Electronic Publishing*, **3** (1), www.press.umich.edu/jep/03-01/kling.html [accessed March 2004].

Noll, R. G. and Steinmueller, W. E. (1992) An Economic Analysis of Scientific Journal Prices: preliminary results, *Serials Review*, **18** (1–2), 32–7.

Nowotny, H., Scott, P. and Gibbons, M. (2001) *Re-thinking Science: knowledge and the public in and age of uncertainty*, Cambridge, Polity Press.

Nowotny, H., Scott, P. and Gibbons, M. (2003) Mode 2 Revisited: the new production of knowledge, *Minerva*, **41** (3), 179–94.

Odlyzko, A. (1998) The Economics of Electronic Publishing, *Journal of Electronic Publishing*, **4** (1), www.press.umich.edu/jep/04-01/ [accessed March 2004].

Odlyzko, A. (2002) The Rapid Evolution of Scholarly Communication, *Learned Publishing*, **15** (1), 7–19, www.catchword.com/alpsp/09531513/v15n1/contp1-1.htm [accessed August 2002].

Peek, R. (2003) Could Peer Review Be Wrong? *Information Today*, **20** (4), www.infotoday.com/it/apr03/peek.shtml [accessed May 2003].

Rowland, F. (2002) *The Peer Review Process: a report to the JISC Scholarly Communications Group*, www.jisc.ac.uk/uploaded_documents/rowland.pdf [accessed April 2004].

Singer, P. (2000) When Shall We Be Free? *Journal of Electronic Publishing*, **6** (2), www.press.umich.edu/jep/06-02/singer.html [accessed March 2004].

Smith, A. P. (2000) The Journal as an Overlay on Preprint Databases, *Learned Publishing*, **13** (1), 43–8. www.ingentaselect.com/alpsp/09531513/v13n1/contp1-1.htm [accessed March 2004].

SQW (2003) *Economic Analysis of Scientific Research Publishing*. A report commissioned by the Wellcome Trust, www.wellcome.ac.uk/scipublishing [accessed March 2004].

Steele, C. (2003) Death of the Book?, Paper presented at *Death of the Book?: Challenges and Opportunities for Scholarly Publishing*, National Maritime Museum, Sydney, March 7–8, www.humanities.org.au/NSCF/bookfuture/futureofbook.htm [accessed August 2003].

Stiglitz, J. E. (1999) Knowledge in the Modern Economy. In *Economics of the Knowledge Driven Economy, Conference Proceedings*, Department of Trade and Industry, www.dti.gov.uk/comp/economiccontents.htm [accessed March 2004].

Suber, P. (2004) Open Access Builds Momentum, *ARL Bimonthly Report* (232), www.arl.org/newsltr/232/openaccess.html [accessed March 2004].

Van Orsdel, L. and Born, K. (2003) Big Chill on the Big Deal? *Library Journal*, (15 April), 51–6, www.libraryjournal.com/toc/4%2F15%2F2003 [accessed March 2004].

Varian, H. R. (1995) *Pricing Information Goods*, paper presented at Scholarship in the New Information Environment Symposium, Harvard Law School, www.sims.berkeley.edu/~hal/Papers/price-info-goods.pdf [accessed March 2004].

Varian, H. R. (1998) The Future of Electronic Journals, *Journal of Electronic Publishing*, 4 (1), www.press.umich.edu/jep/04-01/varian.html [accessed March 2004].

Watkins, A. (2001) *Electronic Solutions to the Problems of Monograph Publishing*, Library and Information Commission Report 109, The Council for Museums, Archives and Libraries, www.publishers.org.uk [accessed March 2004].

Weber, S. (2001) The Political Economy of Open Source Software. In BRIE-IGCC *Tracking a Transformation: e-commerce and the terms of competition in industries*, Washington DC, Brookings Institution Press, 406–34.

Willinsky, J. (2003) Scholarly Associations and the Economic Viability of Open Access Publishing, *Journal of Digital Information*, 4 (2), http://jodi.ecs.soton.ac.uk/Articles/v04/i02/Willinsky/ [accessed April 2004].

Wyly, B. J. (1998) Competition in Scholarly Publishing? What publisher profits reveal, *ARL* (**200**), www.arl.org/newsltr/200/wyly.html.

Zandonella, C. (2003) Economics of Open Access: supporters of new publishing model still face skepticism about journals' viability, *Scientist*, (22 August), www.biomedcentral.com/news/20030822/02/ [accessed April 2004].

10

Usage statistics: achieving credibility, consistency and compatibility

Peter T. Shepherd

Introduction

In the traditional hard copy publishing environment, usage of publications held in the library was difficult to measure systematically. This meant that meaningful usage statistics were either not available or were insufficiently reliable to form a basis for decisions about the relative value of different publications. In the online publishing environment, it is not only possible to measure usage in a systematic way; it is desirable to do so, from the perspective of the vendor as well as the librarian.

Librarians require online usage statistics to enable them to:

- assess the value of different online products and services
- make better informed purchasing decisions
- plan infrastructure and allocation of resources
- support internal marketing and promotion of library services.

Vendors require online usage statistics to allow them to:

- experiment with new pricing models that reflect the current value of

online publications, rather than the historical hard copy holdings from which they were derived
- assess the relative importance of the different channels by which information reaches the market
- provide editorial support for new product development
- plan infrastructure, improve site design and navigation
- obtain improved market analysis and demographics.

There has been widespread agreement that vendor-generated usage statistics provide the best way forward, but this has not, until now, been translated into the necessary coherent international effort. To be of value, these usage statistics have to satisfy the Three Cs. First, they must be *credible*, and they are not yet generally so, as the recent Association of Research Libraries (2004) e-metrics project has shown. They must also be *consistent*, which they are not currently, due to the lack of standardization of terms and definitions used. Finally, they must be *compatible*, which they are not, due to the wide range of different practices being used by vendors to generate usage statistics. As recently as October 2001, the ARL E-metrics Phase II Report made the following assessment of the situation:

> We conclude that it is largely impossible to compare data across vendors, and we recommend that comparison be limited to data from the same vendors. We believe that the comprehensive standardization of usage statistics and data delivery methods cannot be easily achieved in the short term. (ARL, 2001)

In recent years there has been a growing awareness of the need for an international effort, involving vendors, librarians and intermediaries, to develop acceptable, global standards for measuring online usage. This has resulted in Project COUNTER (Counting Online Usage of NeTworked Electronic Resources), now the leading initiative in the field. This article will focus on COUNTER, but will also highlight the other significant initiatives and progress in online usage statistics. The objective of Project COUNTER is to develop agreed international Codes of Practices governing the recording and exchange of online usage data for different categories of content. Release 1 (published in January 2003) and Release 2 (published in draft form in April 2004) of this Code of Practice both focus on journals and databases. There are two reasons for this. First, these categories of content account for the bulk of library materials budgets. Second, definitions, standards and procedures related to their online delivery are better developed than for other content types. A separate code of practice, covering e-books and e-reference works, is now under development and should be available in draft form before the end of 2004.

It is important to stress that improving the quality of usage statistics benefits publishers and intermediaries as well as librarians. By complying with the COUNTER Code of Practice publishers and intermediaries will be able to provide data to their customers in a format they actually want and this will help them learn more about genuine usage patterns. They will also be able to assess the relative importance of the different channels by which their online products reach the market and to aggregate data for a customer that is using more than one delivery channel. New pricing models for online products are emerging that require vendors to take usage into account; usage data supporting these should be credible. The infrastructure required to support electronic products is sophisticated and costly; access to reliable usage statistics will help publishers make an appropriate allocation of caches, mirror sites, and so on.

Existing initiatives on usage statistics

COUNTER has been built on, and liaises with, a number of important ongoing industry initiatives, which have done much valuable work to define customer requirements for usage statistics from vendors. Most notable in this context are the four described below.

ARL New Measures Initiative

The ARL New Measures Initiative has been set up in response to the following two needs: increasing demand for libraries to demonstrate outcomes and impacts in areas important to the institution, and increasing pressure to maximize use of resources. Of particular interest is the work associated with the e-metrics portion of this initiative, which is an effort to explore the feasibility of defining and collecting data on the use and value of electronic resources.

E-measures project: University of Central England, Centre for Information Research

This project (www.ebase.uce.ac.uk/emeasures/) is designed to support the management of electronic information services in UK higher education institutes. Its objectives are to develop a new set of performance measures for electronic information sources and to pilot these with a view to establishing a new set of standard performance measures.

ICOLC Guidelines for Statistical Measures of Usage of Web-based Information Resources

The International Coalition of Library Consortia (ICOLC) has been in existence since 1996. The Coalition is an international informal group currently comprising over 160 library consortia in North America, Australia, Asia and Africa. ICOLC has developed the Guidelines for Statistical Measures of Usage of Web-based Information Resources. Revised in 2001, the Guidelines specify a set of minimum requirements for usage data, and also provide guidance on privacy, confidentiality, access, delivery and report formats. For additional information, visit www.library.yale.edu/consortia/2001webstats.htm.

NISO Forum on Performance Measures and Statistics for Libraries

The National Information Standards Organization (NISO) held a Forum on Performance Measures and Statistics for Libraries on 15–16 February 2001 to gather information from the library community and key vendors about the best approach to evaluate the NISO Standard Z39.7 on Library Statistics. The forum allowed a diverse group of stakeholders to explore their requirements and vision for describing, measuring, and showing the significance of contemporary library services. A new draft of this standard, which details and defines significant library input and output measures, was released in July 2002. Further information on Standard Z39.7 and on the forum can be found on the NISO website at www.niso.org.

The origins of COUNTER

COUNTER had its genesis in the UK, with the Publisher and Librarian Solutions (PALS) group formed by the Joint Information Systems Committee, the Association of Learned and Professional Society Publishers and the Publishers Association. Under chairman Richard Gedye of Oxford University Press, PALS made considerable progress during 2000 and 2001 in developing the framework and processes that evolved into COUNTER. In March 2002 COUNTER was formally launched, with a fully international steering group, a dedicated project director and a set of clear objectives. The widespread acceptance of COUNTER was clear from the outset, with the ready support of the following organizations and agencies:

- Association of American Publishers
- The Association of Learned and Professional Society Publishers
- Association of Research Libraries
- Association of Subscription Agents and Intermediaries
- Book Industry Communication/EDItEUR (the international group coordinating development of the standards infrastructure for electronic commerce in the book and serials sectors)
- Joint Information Systems Committee
- National Committee on Libraries and Information Science
- National Information Standards Organization
- The Publishers Association
- International Association of Scientific, Technical & Medical Publishers
- United Kingdom Serials Group

With the publication and wide acceptance of Release 1 of the Code of Practice, it was decided that COUNTER required a formal organizational structure to provide a solid basis for long-term development.

Consequently, in August 2003 COUNTER was incorporated as Counter Online Metrics, a not-for-profit company in England. Counter Online Metrics is owned by its members. The organization of Counter Online Metrics is described in more detail later.

Strategy

At its first meeting in March 2002, the COUNTER Steering Group agreed the following objectives for the project in 2002:

* gain industry support for COUNTER
* increase awareness of COUNTER
* deliver Release 1 of the COUNTER Code of Practice.

By the end of 2002 all of the above objectives had been achieved. The project was widely supported from the outset and achieved a high profile through conference presentations, the publication of articles and its website (www.projectCOUNTER.org).

COUNTER has progressed only through the active co-operation of the library and vendor communities. Librarians must specify what they want; vendors must decide what they can deliver. Realistic, if testing, goals were agreed at the outset, and progress toward these goals has been steady. This has, in large measure, been due to the strategy adopted by COUNTER, which has the following elements:

1 Buy-in from both the library and vendor communities: COUNTER has been actively supported by both communities from the beginning, and there is balanced representation from both on the Board of Directors, Executive Committee and International Advisory Board.
2 Start small: the scope of Release 1 of the COUNTER Code of Practice was confined to journals and databases, as these are the two most important online budget items for librarians. The scope of the Code of Practice will be extended in response to user feedback.
3 Start with the basics: the usage reports specified in the Code of Practice deal with simple metrics that are within the grasp of all online journal and database publishers.

4 Compatibility is the goal, not sophistication: it is important that as many publishers as possible are able to comply with the Code of Practice.

5 Be as prescriptive as possible in the Code of Practice: this is important to ensure compatibility among different vendor usage reports.

6 Build on and co-operate with other existing organizations and initiatives; notably the ARL New Measures Initiative, the ICOLC Guidelines for Statistical Measures of Usage of Web-based Information Resources, and NISO Standard Z39.7.

7 Supplement rather than substitute existing, more sophisticated or product-related usage reports.

8 Provide support and advice for vendors and librarians on implementation.

9 Give librarians confidence in the quality of the data by setting standards for auditing that result in credible data without placing an undue burden on vendors.

Developing the Code of Practice

A key target group for COUNTER is the international librarian community. Although they are well represented on the COUNTER Executive Committee, it was also decided that librarians at large should be consulted regularly to ensure that their needs are being met by the project. An opportunity arose to do so when the first draft of the usage reports to be included in Release 1 of the Code of Practice were available in July 2002. These were tested in an online librarian survey conducted through the COUNTER website, to which over 650 librarians worldwide responded. The full results are available on the COUNTER website and this feedback was taken into account in the development of the usage reports eventually included in Release 1. The following points were clear from the results of the survey:

• librarians are seeking a relatively *small* number of *reliable* reports
• usage reports should be made available on a password-controlled website, with e-mail alerts when new data is available
• usage reports must be provided at least monthly, and data should be

updated within two weeks of the end of the reporting period
* usage reports should be provided in an Excel spreadsheet or in a format that can be imported into Excel.

Taking into account the above feedback, Release 1 of the COUNTER Code of Practice was published in January 2003.

Release 1 of the COUNTER Code of Practice

The full text of Release 1 of the COUNTER Code of Practice is freely available on the COUNTER website. It specifies in detail the requirements that vendors must meet to have their usage reports designated COUNTER-compliant. The main features of Release 1 are summarized below.

Definitions of terms used

The Code of Practice contains an extensive list of data elements and other terms used in the usage reports and other parts of the Code. Where possible, existing definitions from NISO, ISO, ARL and other organizations have been used. Among the terms defined are 'vendor', 'aggregator', 'article', 'full-text article', 'search', 'item request', 'consortium' and 'consortium member'. This comprehensive list of definitions is proving to be a useful industry resource and is becoming more and more widely used for purposes not directly related to COUNTER.

Also defined are the protocols to be observed when an aggregator or gateway is involved in the delivery of vendor content to the customer. These protocols are particularly important to avoid duplicate counting of usage by publisher and aggregator in situations where an intermediary aggregator or gateway is involved.

Data processing and auditing

As the way usage records are generated differs from one platform to another, it is impractical to describe all the possible filters used to clean up the data. Instead, the Code of Practice specifies the requirements to be met by the data to be used for building the usage reports. A guiding principle is that only intended usage should be recorded, and all requests that are not intended by the user are removed. To this end, all double clicks on an http link within 10 seconds of each other will be counted as only one request. Where a PDF link is involved, this filter is set at 30 seconds, due to the longer time it takes to render a PDF.

Auditing of vendor usage reports and processes by an approved third party will be a requirement for COUNTER compliance from 2005. Detailed auditing specifications will be made available, along with a list of approved auditors, during 2004.

Usage reports

There are seven usage reports, covering journals and databases, in Release 1 of the COUNTER Code of Practice. These have been divided into Level 1 and Level 2 reports:

- Journal Report 1: number of full-text article requests by month and journal (Level 1)
- Journal Report 2: turnaways by month and journal (this report is only applicable where the user access model is based on a maximum number of concurrent users) (Level 1)
- Journal Report 3: number of item requests by month, journal and page type (Level 2)
- Journal Report 4: total searches by month and collection (Level 2)
- Database Report 1: total searches, sessions and full-text requests by month and database (Level 1)
- Database Report 2: turnaways by month and database (Level 1)
- Database Report 3: referrals by aggregator or gateway (Level 1).

Only Level 1 reports are required for COUNTER compliance, but those vendors who can provide the more detailed Level 2 reports are welcome to do so, and also encouraged to use the COUNTER definitions in any other usage reports they may provide to specific customers. Journal Report 1 is proving to be the most widely implemented of the usage reports and the Release 1 specification for Journal Report 1 is provided in Table 10.1 (overleaf).

Table 10.1 Journal Report 1: number of successful full-text article requests by month and journal

	Print ISSN	Online ISSN	Jan-01	Feb-01	Mar-01	Calendar YTD
Total for all journals			6637	8732	7550	45897
Journal of AA	1212-3131	3225-3123	456	521	665	4532
Journal of BB	9821-3361	2312-8751	203	251	275	3465
Journal of CC	2464-2121	0154-1521	0	0	0	0
Journal of DD	5355-5444	0165-5542	203	251	275	2978

Notes:

1 The 'Total for all journals' line is provided at the top of the table to allow it to be stripped out without disrupting the rest of the table, as the number of journals included may vary from one month to another.
2 Journals for which the number of full-text article requests is zero in every month should be included in Journal Report 1.
3 Full journal name, print ISSN and online ISSN are listed.

Even this relatively simple report is proving a challenge for many vendors to provide, as they must meet the specified format exactly, otherwise it is impossible for librarians to merge or compare reports from different vendors.

Report delivery

Report delivery must conform to the following standards for Release 1:

- Reports must be provided either as a CSV file, as a Microsoft Excel file, or as a file that can be easily imported into Microsoft Excel.
- Reports should be made available on a password-controlled website (accompanied by an e-mail alert when data is updated).
- Reports must be provided at least monthly.
- Data must be updated within four weeks of the end of the reporting period.
- All of last calendar year's data and this calendar year's to date must be supplied.

At the time of writing only a minority of compliant vendors were able to supply all of last calendar year's data, but this archive will grow with time.

Compliance with Release 1

Compliance with the Code of Practice is encouraged in two ways. First, customers are urged to include a clause in all relevant licence agreements specifying that vendors provide usage statistics that are COUNTER-compliant. A standard template for this clause is provided in the Code of Practice. Second, to obtain COUNTER-compliant status for their usage reports vendors are required to sign a formal Declaration of COUNTER Compliance and to allow the COUNTER office to review those of their usage reports that they claim are compliant. These reports are then listed in the register of vendors on the COUNTER website. Only reports listed there may be regarded as being COUNTER-compliant. During 2004 vendor usage reports are being monitored at five library test sites, which are providing useful feedback to individual vendors and to COUNTER; this is helping improve implementation. To maintain COUNTER-compliant status from 2005, vendors' reports will have to be audited by an independent auditor. The auditing standards and processes are being developed in the course of 2004.

By the end of April 2004, 30 vendors had achieved COUNTER-compliant status. Many of the major journal and database publishers as well as intermediaries are now compliant, including the American Association for the Advancement of Science, the American Chemical Society, Blackwell Publishing, EBSCO, Elsevier, HighWire Press, ISI, Oxford University Press, Nature Publishing Group, Springer and Wiley. Already over 50% of the annual output of articles covered by the Science Citation Index is in COUNTER-compliant journals, and this proportion is growing monthly.

Feedback on Release 1

Following publication of Release 1 feedback was sought from the library, intermediary and vendor community. Already there is evidence that COUNTER-compliant usage statistics are beginning to be used by librarians to assess the value of online journals and databases. To obtain feedback in a more structured way a number of focus groups were held during the second half of 2003. The feedback obtained was clear and useful. The following strong recommendations were of particular significance:

1 *Slow down the pace of development and implementation of Release 2 until more feedback is obtained on Release 1.* Given that most vendors only began to become compliant during the second half of 2003, librarians have not yet had sufficient experience with the Release 1 usage reports to comment on how they work in practice. It was decided, therefore, to postpone the implementation of Release 2 for one year. Release 1 will now remain the valid version of the Code of Practice until January 2005.

2 *Confine the Code of Practice to a set of basic usage reports that make it easy for a large number of vendors to comply with and provide librarians with the core data they really need.* This has been a strong request from librarians and vendors alike. Librarians want to develop a basic set of metrics derived from reliable usage statistics, not to be overwhelmed with data. Some vendors are alarmed at the prospect of COUNTER requirements becoming ever more complex, demanding and expensive; this will not be the case.

3 *Develop a separate code of practice for e-books and e-reference works.* It was agreed that expanding the current Code of Practice to cover more content types would make it too complex for users. It will be less confusing to create a separate code of practice for e-books and e-reference works, even though this may have elements in common with the current releases for journals and databases .

4 *Post draft versions of future releases on the website for comment in order to make the process more transparent.* Release 2 has been published in draft form on the COUNTER website. Comments were accepted until 30 September 2004.

Release 2 of the COUNTER Code of Practice

The draft of Release 2 was published on the COUNTER website in April

2004. It is planned to publish the final version of Release 2 of the COUNTER Code of Practice in January 2005 and this will become the definitive version in January 2006. Until then Release 1 remains the Code of Practice with which vendors should comply.

Release 2 of the COUNTER Code of Practice has been developed with input from librarian focus groups held during the second half of 2003, from the COUNTER International Advisory Board and from other sources. The draft text of Release 2 has been approved by the COUNTER Executive Committee, who decided that it will continue to focus on journals and databases (and that a separate COUNTER code of practice should be developed during 2004 for e-books and e-reference works).

Features of Release 2

To avoid confusion, the original format and structure of Release 1 has been retained as far as possible. The major changes in Release 2 are as follows.

1 The complete list of definitions of terms used has been moved from Section 3 to an appendix to the Code of Practice. A subset of those definitions that are specific to the usage reports included in Release 2 has been extracted from this list and is published in Section 3 of the Code of Practice.
2 There are some minor modifications to the format of the Release 1 usage reports and one new report, Journal Report 1a: Number of Successful Full-text Requests in HTML and PDF Formats, has been added.

Examples of the modified existing Journal Report 1 and the new Journal Report 1a are provided in Tables 10.2 and 10.3 on pages 202 and 203.

Table 10.2   Journal Report 1: number of successful full-text article requests by month and journal

Journal Report 1 <Criteria> Date run: Yyyy-mm-dd	Publisher	Print ISSN	Online ISSN	Jan-2001	Feb-2001	Mar-2001	Total
Total for all journals				6637	8732	7550	45897
Journal of AA		1212-3131	3225-3123	456	521	665	4532
Journal of BB		9821-3361	2312-8751	203	251	275	3465
Journal of CC		2464-2121	0154-1521	0	0	0	0
Journal of DD		5355-5444	0165-5542	203	251	275	2978

Notes:

1 For 'criteria' specify, for example, the organizational level to which the usage reports refer, e.g. 'institution', 'department'.

2 The 'Total for all journals' line is provided at the top of the table to allow it to be stripped out without disrupting the rest of the table, as the number of journals included may vary from one month to another.

3 Journals for which the number of full-text article requests is zero in every month should be included in Journal Report 1, except where an aggregator or gateway is responsible for recording and reporting the usage.

4 Full journal name, print ISSN and online ISSN are listed.

Table 10.3 Journal Report 1a: number of successful full-text requests in HTML and PDF formats

Journal Report 1a								
<Criteria>								
Date run: Yyyy-mm-dd								
Journal Name	Publisher	Print ISSN	Online ISSN	Page Type	Jan- 2001	Feb- 2001	Mar- 2001	Total
Total for all journals				Full-text PDF requests	2876	3793	3329	26424
Total for all journals				Full-text HTML requests	3201	4392	3982	27902
Journal of AA		1212- 3131	3225- 3123	Full-text PDF requests	621	670	598	4657
Journal of AA		1212- 3131	3225- 3123	Full-text HTML requests	322	420	543	4433

Notes:
1. For 'criteria' specify, for example, the organizational level to which the usage reports refer, e.g. 'institution', 'department'.
2. Full journal name, print ISSN and Online ISSN are listed.

The Level 2 usage reports from Release 1 (Journal Report 3 and Journal Report 4) have been moved to Appendix F to Release 2. These more detailed reports are not a requirement for COUNTER compliance, but are provided by several vendors and are valued by many customers. By including these reports in an appendix we want to provide those vendors who can deliver more detailed usage statistics with a COUNTER-compliant standard that they can apply.

The protocols to be used for recording and reporting usage when an intermediary aggregator or gateway is involved have been collected together in the new Table 10.2. The objective of these protocols is to avoid duplication of counting by the publisher that owns the content and the aggregator/gateway that provides access to it.

A detailed specification for the auditing standards and procedures that will be implemented from 2005, is included in Release 2.

COUNTER organization and membership

To ensure that COUNTER will be viable in the longer term, and will continue to serve the publishing, library and intermediary communities, in August 2004 it was set up as an independent, not-for profit company in England. Known as COUNTER Online Metrics, it is governed by a six member board of directors, chaired by Richard Gedye of Oxford University Press. An executive committee, reporting to the board, is responsible for the management of COUNTER. The 14 members of the executive committee represent the international publisher, intermediary and library communities. In addition, there is an international advisory board of over 30 experts from the same communities. The memberships of the board of directors and the executive committee are given below. These are also published on the COUNTER website, along with the international advisory board:

COUNTER Online Metrics: Board of Directors

Richard Gedye (Chair)	Oxford University Press, UK
Christine Fyfe	Leicester University, UK
David Goodman	Long Island University, USA
Ann Okerson	Yale University, UK
Peter Shepherd	Project Director, UK
Eefke Smit	Elsevier, The Netherlands

COUNTER Online Metrics: Executive Committee

Richard Gedye (Chair)	Oxford University Press, UK
Marthyn Borghuis	Elsevier, The Netherlands
Roger Brown	GlaxoSmithKline, UK
Phil Davis	Cornell University, USA

Christine Fyfe	Leicester University, UK
David Goodman	Long Island University, USA
Timo Hannay	Nature Publishing Group, UK
Arnold Hirshon	NELINET, USA
Terry Hulbert	Institute of Physics Publishing, UK
Tony Kidd	Glasgow University, UK
Oliver Pesch	EBSCO
Eileen Shanbrom	Chemical Abstracts Service, USA

COUNTER Online Metrics is owned by its members, and from 2004 its only source of income is its member subscriptions. Publishers, intermediaries, libraries, consortia and industry organizations are all eligible for full, voting membership at the following rates in 2003: publisher £500, intermediary £500, library £250, industry organization £250 and consortium £500.

By the end of March 2004 there were 130 COUNTER members in all categories. Our target for 2004 is 150, so we are already close to our target. Our goal for 2005 is to recruit 200 members, as this will ensure a solid base of funding for the future. COUNTER's funding requirements are modest. We need around US$100,000 per annum to support all our activities.

The benefits of full COUNTER membership include:

- the right to vote at the annual general meeting on the direction and management of COUNTER, including appointments to the board of directors
- regular bulletins on the progress of COUNTER
- advice on implementation of COUNTER.

As a lower price alternative to the above, non-voting affiliate membership is available to libraries at £100. Library affiliates will receive the regular member bulletins on the progress of COUNTER.

Further information on membership, as well as application forms, may be found on the COUNTER website.

Conclusion: 2004 and beyond

In 2004 the main objectives for COUNTER are to:

- increase the number of vendors complying with the COUNTER Code of Practice
- obtain feedback on the draft of Release 2: using this feedback, finalize Release 2, ready for publication in January 2005
- define the audit process and complete the list of approved auditors
- prepare the first draft of a COUNTER code of practice for e-books and e-reference works
- reach the target of 150 members of COUNTER.

These objectives are proving testing to meet. The COUNTER Code of Practice contains very detailed specifications that must be adhered to: usage statistics will only be of real value to customers if the majority of vendors can produce and deliver them to the required standards. Even the basic set of statistics required for COUNTER compliance are proving a challenge to many vendors and we are working actively with them to ensure full compliance. It is important that customers and vendors are realistic about what can be achieved in the short term.

Then there are books. Our experience with journals and databases has given us the confidence that COUNTER is now ready to develop a new code of practice that will cover e-books and e-reference works. This will, we hope, bring usage statistics that are credible, compatible and consistent to these product lines.

Looking further ahead, there is already a considerable body of literature which demonstrates not only that journal articles are well used, but are also a major stimulus for creativity, innovation and new product development. The work of Tenopir and King (1996, 1999, 2000) provides solid evidence for this. The availability of more comprehensive and reliable usage statistics will shed further light on the value and utility of journal articles. Jerry Cowhig (2002), Managing Director of the Institute of Physics Publishing, has argued that, given the well known limitations of citation data, usage statistics could provide another metric for publishing activity. He pointed out that properly audited usage statistics would provide a credible alternative perspective on the quality and value of individual articles and journals. COUNTER, if widely adopted, has the potential to play a significant role in this.

COUNTER's founding sponsors

During 2002 and 2003 COUNTER was supported by contributions from its founding sponsors. COUNTER is deeply grateful to these sponsors, listed below, whose generous financial contributions have enabled this project to commence its work. We salute their vision, commitment and support.

American Institute of Physics
Association of American Publishers/Professional & Scholarly Publishing Division
Association of College and Research Libraries
The Association of Learned & Professional Society Publishers
Association of Research Libraries
Association of Subscription Agents and Intermediaries
Blackwell Publishing
BMJ Publishing Group
EBSCO
Elsevier
HighWire Press
Ingenta
Institute of Physics Publishing
International Association of Scientific, Technical & Medical Publishers
International Council for Scientific and Technical Information
Joint Information Systems Committee
JSTOR
Lippincott, Williams & Wilkins
Nature Publishing Group
New England Journal of Medicine
OCLC
Oxford University Press
ProQuest

The Publishers Association
Taylor & Francis Group
Thieme Publishing Group
United Kingdom Serials Group

References

Association of Research Libraries (2001) Measures and Statistics for Research Library Networked Services: procedures and issues, www.arl.org/stats/newmeas/emetrics/phasetwopreface.pdf.

Association of Research Libraries (2004) *E-metrics: measures for electronic resources*, www.arl.org/stats/newmeas/emetrics/index.html.

Cowhig, J. (2002) What's Wrong with Impact Factors? And is there an alternative?, Presentation at Charleston Conference, Charleston SC, November.

King, D. W. and Tenopir, C. (1999) Evolving Journal Costs: implications for publishers, libraries and readers, *Learned Publishing*, **12** (4), 251–8.

Tenopir, C. and King, D. W. (1996) Setting the Record Straight on Journal Publishing: myth vs. reality, *Library Journal*, **121** (15 March), 32–5.

Tenopir, C. and King, D. W. (2000) *Towards Electronic Journals: realities for scientist, librarians and publishers*, Washington DC, Special Libraries Association.

Index

Page numbers in *italics* indicate references to figures.